ISBN 978-1-330-51366-8
PIBN 10072093

1 MONTH OF
FREE
READING

at

www.ForgottenBooks.com

By purchasing this book you are eligible for one month membership to ForgottenBooks.com, giving you unlimited access to our entire collection of over 1,000,000 titles via our web site and mobile apps.

To claim your free month visit: www.forgottenbooks.com/free72093

English
Français
Deutsche
Italiano
Español
Português

www.forgottenbooks.com

Mythology Photography **Fiction**
Fishing Christianity **Art** Cooking
Essays Buddhism Freemasonry
Medicine **Biology** Music **Ancient**
Egypt Evolution Carpentry Physics
Dance Geology **Mathematics** Fitness
Shakespeare **Folklore** Yoga Marketing
Confidence Immortality Biographies
Poetry **Psychology** Witchcraft
Electronics Chemistry History **Law**
Accounting **Philosophy** Anthropology
Alchemy Drama Quantum Mechanics
Atheism Sexual Health **Ancient History**
Entrepreneurship Languages Sport
Paleontology Needlework Islam
Metaphysics Investment Archaeology
Parenting Statistics Criminology
Motivational

OUR

LIBERAL MOVEMENT

IN THEOLOGY

*CHIEFLY AS SHOWN IN RECOLLECTIONS OF THE
HISTORY OF UNITARIANISM IN
NEW ENGLAND*

BEING

A CLOSING COURSE OF LECTURES GIVEN IN THE
HARVARD DIVINITY SCHOOL

BY

JOSEPH HENRY ALLEN

Lecturer on Ecclesiastical History in Harvard University

HONORARY MEMBER OF THE (UNITARIAN) SUPREME CONSISTORY OF TRANSYL-
VANIA, AUTHOR OF "HEBREW MEN AND TIMES," "CHRISTIAN
HISTORY IN ITS THREE GREAT PERIODS," &c.

THIRD EDITION

BOSTON
ROBERTS BROTHERS
1892

UNIVERSITY PRESS:
JOHN WILSON AND SON, CAMBRIDGE.

PREFATORY NOTE.

THE following correspondence sufficiently explains the circumstances which have led to the publication of this volume : —

DIVINITY SCHOOL, HARVARD UNIVERSITY,
CAMBRIDGE, May 10, 1882.

DEAR SIR, — We, the undersigned, wishing to possess the Lectures on the "Liberal Movement in Theology," recently delivered before the Divinity School of Harvard University, in a more permanent form, express our earnest desire for the publication of the same.

Very truly yours,

H. PRICE COLLIER,
JOHN A. TUNIS,
CHARLES F. RUSSELL,
Committee for the School.

CAMBRIDGE, May 14, 1882.

MY DEAR FRIENDS, — Your very kind letter gives me the opportunity, which I am delighted to embrace, of leaving with you a memento of the four years I have passed, most agreeably, in connection with this School.

Trusting that you may all have the privilege of doing your share in that noble and most interesting work, of which I have attempted to trace some of the antecedents and conditions, I am, with the sincerest regard,

Your friend,

J. H. ALLEN.

These circumstances will explain, if they do not justify, a more personal tone in these Lectures than would belong to a purely historical or critical review. In fact, the value of the volume, if it has any, turns mainly on its being, in good part, made up of reminiscences and personal testimony. It is, besides, in some sense the final link in a series, of which "Hebrew Men and Times" makes the first, and the third, under the title "The Middle Age," is now in press.

I will only add, that some passages may perhaps be recognized as having appeared here and there in print. In particular, most of the article on Unitarianism in a pamphlet entitled "Three Phases of Modern Theology" has been included here; and the Lecture on "The Gospel of Liberalism" is substantially the same with the Address to the Alumni of this School delivered in 1880.

By the kindness of Dr. Hedge I am permitted to add in the form of an Appendix, with some revision and addition by his hand, his recent Memorial Address on Bellows and Emerson.

HARVARD DIVINITY SCHOOL,
CAMBRIDGE, June 10, 1882.

CONTENTS.

OUR
LIBERAL MOVEMENT IN THEOLOGY.

I.

ANTECEDENTS.

THERE are two ways of looking at any form of religious thought that appears in history. One is, to see it as a fixed type of opinion; the other is, to see it as a phase in the development of religious truth. One sees it in the distinct outline it has taken in creed or symbol, as set forth by its recognized interpreters; the other sees it as one stage of a movement that began long before there was any record of it, and will continue so long as men think at all seriously on religious things.

The former way has been much more common. It corresponds with the *absolute* temper in which religious opinion has generally been held, and with that aim at absolute truth, and the faultless statement of it, which men have thought their highest duty. What is naturally fluent, and by the very laws of thought must change continually as the bearings of all our knowledge change, men have continually endeavored to fix in rigid forms that could not be altered or lost.

So we find the history of religious thought chiefly made up of the recital of creeds, with the story of the controversies that have grown out of them, or else have been reconciled in them. It is even taken for granted that every religious movement must perforce express itself in such a creed. To this day the question is asked, "What do Unitarians believe?" — just as if that question were at all relevant, as touching the movement which the various phases of Unitarian opinion represent. Unitarians themselves, in entire good faith, are trying to this day to find some statement or form of declaration broad enough to include them all, and precise enough to mean something when it has cancelled all they differ in; while in equal good faith they assure the world that no one is to be held responsible for that or any other statement that can be made.

Now it is not quite satisfactory to say, as many do, that Unitarians simply guard, with more than common jealousy, their right as Protestants to private judgment: in other words, that they are not only "Unitarian" Christians, but also "Liberal" Christians. This has never been felt fairly to meet the case. Inquirers think they have a right to expect more; believers feel they have a right to assume more. And many attempts have been made to state the Unitarian position with authority. But when we come to examine these attempts we are apt to be struck with two things: first, that they have a certain apologetic tone, as if the main point were not to say frankly just what the writer himself thinks, but rather to show that Unitarians are pretty good Christians after all,—in short, to come as near the popular creed as may be without quite hitting it; and secondly, that they are mostly made up of details, or brief formulas of religious phraseology, or points of Bible-interpretation, — notoriously wide apart from the opinions of many who rate themselves as Unitarians, and who stand in general esteem as well as anybody among them.

I have spoken of one way of looking at the matter, — that which we may call the sectarian or dogmatic way. The other is what, for distinction, we may call the scientific way: that, namely, which we take as students of the laws of thought, or of religious development in a broad sense. In other words, it is the history of a Movement we are to study, not the attitude of a Sect.

Not that Unitarianism has generally been true in thought to what it is in fact. It is much easier to figure itself as a sect than as a movement away from all sects,—from a dogmatic towards a purely scientific conception of religious truth. But this latter view is that which we shall have to take, if we would do any justice to its history.

In particular it is necessary, to explain the many inconsistencies in that history. I do not say, to apologize for them. I have not the least intention of saying a word in apology. I may perhaps have to speak of a good many things as a critic, but certainly not as an apologist. In a very near and special sense Unitarianism is my birthright, which it would be dishonorable as well as painful to disown. As to that, I am entirely content with the position in which

Providence has placed us; and I do not think we need to look far along the line of our history to find abundant matter of pride — if we choose to indulge it — in our antecedents and our record. That, among the rest, it will be my business to show if I can.

The historical view which I propose to take is necessary, then, for justice to the Unitarian movement, whether as regards its opponents or its friends. On one hand, you would get from the written statements of Unitarians a notion that, however it may be with their opinions, their method differs from the Orthodox only by a hair's breadth, being just a little more precise, rigid, and scrupulous in its exposition of particular passages and texts, while avoiding mystery and bringing poetry down to the level of plain sense.

On the other hand, a broad popular judgment, which it cannot conciliate or escape, holds Unitarianism responsible for a radical drift, thinly covered by conservative phrases, or hidden from itself, perhaps, by the mist of pious feeling. It is very important for our own honesty and self-respect that we should know how much of this is true. Unitarianism has educated, it has also enlisted, a great variety of opinion: is there any real unity behind this diversity? It claims to be one form of religious doctrine; namely, the Unity of the Godhead: but does its name after all mean anything more than "unity of spirit" among its adherents, — if, indeed, so much as that? And these are questions to which it seems impossible to give any other answer than an historical answer. They must be met by the record, not of opinion, but of fact.

Moreover, in no one thing has the independence claimed by Unitarians been more freely asserted than in their criticism of themselves and of one another. This, in fact, is one standing charge of weakness in them. Still, in matters of this sort, honesty is a good deal more important than strength, especially than a false show of strength. It is rather to their credit that there is little factitious unity among them. Their efforts after unity have been not much in the way of suppression and exclusion; mostly by way of merging outspoken differences in a common sentiment or a common work. Their very title some of them have disowned in the name of a broader Christianity or a broader humanity. This breadth, this vagueness, has been inevitable, under the condition of things they stood in. But it is mere justice to acknowledge the fact of it, with whatever credit it may deserve; at least to recognize its value in attempting the special problem that had to be met.

For that problem will appear more radical and difficult in proportion as we feel the fundamental change we undergo in passing from a dogmatic to a scientific method in religious things.

I will not anticipate here what will appear more plainly as we get farther on; except to say that, far from accepting the methods of physical science, it is deliverance from them we seek, in establishing those of what we may rightly call religious science. The question of method is far deeper than that of any application or result of a given method; and a change of theological method means a great revolution of religious thought. That such a revolution — distantly

heralded by the controversies of the Reformation —
is in full sweep in the religious world, I must take
for granted, not seek to prove. I have only to say
further, by way of preface, that Unitarianism could
hold no more honorable historical position than as
consciously aiding in that larger movement, and do
no more honorable task than to help, ever so little,
towards that higher intellectual and spiritual life
which it betokens.

The name Unitarian, it is perhaps needless to say,
has been given by general consent to that style of
theology which is unable to see, or refuses to see,
a distinction of persons in the Godhead, whatever
that may be interpreted to mean. In this sense,
Mahometans are called, and very justly called, a
Unitarian sect, or rather a vast group of Unitarian
sects. They have even been called a Christian sect,
since they hold Jesus to have been one of the six
great prophets, along with Adam, Noah, Abraham,
Moses, and Mahomet. And, in fact, their indignant
and intolerant proclamation of the divine unity was
aimed at the fantastic corruptions of Eastern Christianity quite as much as at the multitude of Arabian
idols.

But that is simply a term of intellectual definition.
As we understand the word, it defines those who
belong within the broad circle of Christendom, and
not to any of the outlying circles. Those who hold
it generally insist very positively — even if somewhat
dryly, and with a lack of Orthodox reverence and
fervor — on the absolute supremacy, nay, the absolute
perfection of Jesus as a divinely appointed teacher

and guide; and those who do not state it quite so dogmatically nevertheless hold that the gospel proclaimed by Jesus contains the key and the inspiration of that vast religious and moral force known as Christianity, and is in fact the solution, from the highest point of view, of the knottiest problems that touch human character and conduct. So that the bleak monotheism of Mahometanism does not come into the account, any more than the philosophical monotheism of Plato and Cicero, in a fair historical view of what the name Unitarian implies.

Again, not only the earliest Christian belief — that of the first disciples and of the New Testament — was really (as we think) unitarian; but, after the doctrine of Christ's divinity became dominant, there were many sects called heretical, which held various forms of unitarianism, or near approaches to it, — Sabellian, Arian, Nestorian, and the rest, — which there is no need to consider here, since they were soon overborne by the immense sweep of the current of church belief, or else suppressed by the heavy hand of church authority. Except for mere antiquarian curiosity, we have to do only with those forms of it which have arisen in modern times, — that is, since the controversies of the Reformation.

It happens, too, that that form of it which arose during the Reformation period has had very little effect on later opinion; at least on that current of opinion which sets towards us. There were Unitarians of the school of Socinus, learned, critical, honest, devout; but a more scrupulous orthodoxy succeeded in turning their name into a byword of reproach.

The name Socinian has been often cast against modern Unitarians; and has always been disclaimed by them, as belonging to a phase of rationalism which they had nothing to do with, while they were quite free to profess honor and respect to the founders of that school. Again, there has been a distinct Unitarian tradition eastward in Europe, forming a current (it would seem) quite independent of western opinion, whose names of honor are the Polish brethren, and the careful scholars of Transylvania, only lately known to us by personal communication. With these, too, our inquiry has nothing practically to do.

Still further, to narrow our field within easy compass, quite a number of religious bodies exist which are really unitarian in belief, though they do not take this as their recognized name, and stand outside this particular movement. Thus the Swedenborgians acknowledge only one Lord, and him only in the person of Christ. The Universalists are generally unitarian in theology; but with a powerful denominational organization of their own, and starting, in their doctrinal history, with a view of the atonement, and of its universal efficacy, which parts them still more widely from Unitarians than from the Orthodox sects. The "Christian" sect is unitarian; but on the basis of a rigid scripturalism, and with antecedents that separate it completely in spirit from what is historically known as such. And among the forms in which Orthodoxy is held by liberal and cultivated minds, there are some which can hardly be distinguished, in any fair analysis, from a very common phase of the Unitarian belief.

Now I am not dealing with the matter philosophically or dogmatically, but only historically; and so it is necessary to set aside all these outlying forms, though some of them are extremely interesting and important. I have to do only with that distinct series of antecedents which has determined the existence of Unitarianism as we know it, and has shaped the character of its belief. And these antecedents do not carry us, at present, beyond England and America. And besides, as Unitarianism has had quite a different history in these two countries, I shall refer, very briefly only, to a point or two of the history of opinion in England before coming to that which really concerns ourselves.

The names of Milton, Locke, and Newton are frequently cited as the three great early glories of English unitarianism. Let us stop a moment and see what those great names stand for.

Milton's unitarianism was first clearly brought to light in his work on Christian Doctrine, of which the manuscript was found iu 1825. It shows that the reflection of his later years, turned upon the great mass of sacred learning he had gathered in his laborious life, led him, on grounds of simple interpretation of the Bible, to an opinion — a certain qualified Arianism — strange and daring then, though as different from what would be called scientific criticism now as from the high Calvinistic orthodoxy of his younger days.

The names of Locke and Newton show that the unitarian opinion — held by them in a very grave and reverent temper, widely removed from radical dissent

— made part of that great movement of reason and science which dates from their day. No names were or perhaps are held in so high honor by the average English mind as those two. Their influence was immense in their own day and after, and is a strong force even now. Newton's name is even reverently cited by Englishmen as that of the greatest intellect ever created, and probably, all things considered, the greatest man. Locke, more than any one else, guided the broad movement of English speculation, as it has swept on down to our own time. He did not give his name to any school in theology professedly unitarian, though his own opinion lay that way. But his defence of " The Reasonableness of Christianity " brought religion directly to the bar of reason and argument, away from the tribunal of church authority and dogmatism. The great rationalistic theologians of the English Church followed his lead, — at their head Samuel Clarke, whose orthodoxy was as liberal and easy as that of the devouter school of Unitarians now. In short, he has as distinctly the repute of being an Arian as Milton has, — that is, owning a Christ above all ages and before all worlds, which is also a favorite form of the elder unitarian speculation.

But it was not so much in the Church as outside the Church that the rationalistic movement in theology was strongest. There sprang up early in the last century a remarkable controversy, which has come down with something of an ill name to our own time. I mean the attack on the popular theology made by the English Deists. They were not, any of them, very able men, or very eminent scholars, by the standard of the present day, or even of their own. But they made a great noise in the theological world, and it will sometimes happen that some zealous preachers even now go out of their way to kick the dead body of their opinions, and to dye their obscure reputation with a little deeper shade of prejudice.

And they had indirectly a very powerful effect. They compelled the church theology to stand on its defence with the weapons of free and open debate, — an immense advantage every way. Moreover, by a reaction from the excessive hardness and dryness of this reasoning process, and the encouragement it gave to the worldly temper of the established Church, there came up into history that great heat and flame of Methodism, which has been in some ways the most remarkable and powerful force in Protestantism for the last hundred and forty years. With the immense power and skill of its organization, with the fervors of its piety, with its active missionary zeal, with its wonderful hold upon the rudest classes of all, and the hardest to reach through religious sympathy, Methodism was one of the indirect results of the rationalizing spirit that had issued in the deistical controversy, though by way of antagonism and re-coil.

But I am not giving a history of religion generally, or of that controversy in particular; and so I will only add, that when Christianity was driven by it to appeal to the bar of learning, it chanced that the one eminent scholar who did most to refute the asser-tions of the Deists, and to satisfy the English mind on the ground of history, was the eminent Unitarian scholar, Lardner, whose great work in defence of historical Christianity is a standard to this day. I do not say how far his argument satisfies the scientific thinkers and historical students of our time, who have shifted their ground a good deal from that of a hundred years ago. I only say that, when modern Unitarianism came to take shape, and began to be known under its own name, it was as a defence of Christianity on the grounds of reason against the attacks of reason. That gave it a precise, dry, accurate, and rationalizing temper from the start, from which it has never been quite free, — the very antipodes of Methodism in temper and doctrine, so far as such a thing could be within the recognized boundaries of Christian belief.

Thus the Unitarian movement which we date from was born of reason, and appealed to reason from its birth. One other thing, and I have done with this historical phase of it. Reason in those days meant not merely argument against superstition, or enthusiasm, or false theology: it also meant assertion of the rights of man. It was a time of revolution. Jefferson was a unitarian of those days, of the more daring and rationalistic school that sympathized with French opinion, yet in his way a serious and even a devout thinker. His assertions of human right, the "glittering generalities" which he put in the Declaration of Independence, were of the gospel of humanity of that day; and by none was that gospel taken up with more ardor than by the English Unitarians, reasoners and independent thinkers as they were.

The most brilliant disciples of that new gospel

were the group of enthusiastic young poets, full then of
socialistic and humanitarian dreams, — Wordsworth,
Coleridge, and Southey : Coleridge even figured once
as a Unitarian preacher. This great revolutionary
drift — part reason, part sentiment — called out the
wrath and alarm of the saviours of society in those
days, Edmund Burke at their head, whose great genius bent from its path to insult and reject a petition
for justice presented in the name of the feeble sect of
Unitarians. His splendid harangues on the philosophy of politics could admit nothing but eloquent
scorn for anything that challenged, however humbly,
the imperial majesty of Church and State.

A religious movement, like a political revolution,
takes its character from what has gone before it, and
must be studied in its antecedents quite as much as
in its events and symptoms. For that reason it was
necessary to show how modern Unitarianism — in
however small and unnoticed a way — was an outgrowth of the general development of thought in the
last century in England. In reality, it probably
existed as much inside as outside the established
Church, in that great body of " latitude-men," or lat-
itudinarians of a scientific, free-thinking, and somewhat worldly habit of mind, who were at once the
intellectual glory and the spiritual discredit of that
Church. I do not see why Paley, the most eminent
churchman of one hundred years ago, was not as
much a unitarian, to all intents and purposes, as
Price or Lardner.

But we are dealing with the body specifically
known as such ; and that was necessarily a dissenting

body. How it was historically connected with that large and most honorable body of Nonconformists, whose dissent was one of the noblest acts of deliberate self-sacrifice on record, and how in particular it claims to this day Presbyterian traditions and inheritance, it would take more historical detail than I have time for, to explain. Just at present we have to do only with one or two characteristics which those antecedents left as a peculiar stamp upon it.

The two points thus most strongly marked in its history are: first, that it was a movement of Reason in sympathy with the scientific spirit; and second, that it was a movement of Right, in sympathy with the revolutionary spirit. These two characteristics it will be necessary to keep in mind; because, however disguised, they have marked its history ever since, and because they explain the two sorts of controversy that have always been going on more or less in the Unitarian ranks. The two happened to be represented, at the time I am speaking of (nearly a hundred years ago), by the two very distinguished names of Priestley and Price. The first, a gentle, brave, able man, with high repute as a chemist at that day, was driven off by a mob in Birmingham, about 1790, and spent the last years of his life in Pennsylvania. Price, of a more speculative and radical temper, was especially honored with the hostility of Edmund Burke, in the zeal of his repugnance, horror, and hate against the French Revolution.

With such forerunners and defenders as these, Unitarianism soon took the character by which it has been best known, — as *a system of morality and piety founded on the authority of a divine revelation in the New Testament.* This revelation was accepted in all sincerity for its practical uses ; and the only test of its efficacy or truth was held to be its practical effect on the life. At the same time, it was interpreted as nearly by principles of pure reason as could be, without forfeiting its distinctive character as revelation. This, it did not enter into the religious mind of that generation to deny. The Deists of England and the French philosophers — including such disciples of theirs as Thomas Paine — it repudiated as distinctly and almost as indignantly as did the more orthodox sects.

The real character of the Unitarian body was a quiet, unostentatious, domestic, and very genuine piety ; a wholesome, sound, perhaps rather commonplace morality ; with very little of what would be called emotion, enthusiasm, or the more ardent phases of the religious life. Coleridge says that when he was a Unitarian he used to preach sermons on political economy, and rather implies that that was the fashion of the day. But, in point of fact, there was a solid religious background of Unitarian thinking. Its acceptance of the Christian revelation was quite positive and explicit, though as far as possible from anything speculative or mystical. Revelation, to Unitarians, was a foundation divinely laid, and beyond question of man's reason, on which the human structure of common-sense and morality was to be built. Reason should go as far as reason could without disturbing that foundation. And all that is peculiar in the Unitarian system of belief, or style of reasoning, follows naturally and easily enough from that one thing.

To begin with : all speculative inquiries about the existence of God, the immortal life of the soul, and the foundation of duty were superseded by the very simple and downright theory of revelation accepted by the Unitarians. The miraculous narrative of the Bible being once taken as proved, all the rest followed as matter of course. The miracles themselves, accepted as facts, proved the existence of a God who acted upon human affairs personally and directly, and from motives which could easily be inferred and explained to the common mind. The resurrection of Jesus — that and that alone, verified as a fact of history — was the sufficient, the only, the unanswerable proof of man's immortality ; the more valid, because Jesus was not God but a man. The positive declarations of the Ten Commandments and the Sermon on the Mount were the real foundation of authority and sanction of moral duty. The definite warnings and predictions of the Parables, of some of the Epistles, and of the Book of Revelation, were the real and only ground of anticipating any divine judgment of right and wrong. Even the details of history were held in the early Unitarian schools of exposition, to be precisely and accurately predicted by the Hebrew prophets and in the visions of St. John the Divine. Priestley, as complete a rationalist in temper as ever was, goes to work as sincerely as any Adventist, to make the poetry of the Apocalypse correspond with the events of modern history.

I have been thus explicit on this point, because it

was held with great positiveness, and is that from which modern Unitarianism dates, however far its criticism or its speculation may have wandered since. Taking it, too, for a point of departure, it will be easier to follow the changes which have come about in the course of time; and easier to measure the justice of the charges which have generally been made upon the system.   As to that moderate or qualified supernaturalism, there was as much unanimity and heartiness of belief in it among the early Unitarians as can be found among any believers in any foundation of any creed.   The real characteristics of the movement came out in the structure which was built upon it.

In the first place, it was characteristic of that movement to put as *reasonable* an interpretation on the language of the Bible as it would bear; and so it really broke ground in the direction of a rationalism which it honestly disowned.   As a matter of course, it took the reasonable explanation of such dogmas as the trinity, the deity of Christ, the atonement, and so on.   It refused to accept any mysteries on these matters: "Where mystery begins religion ends," it was wont to say.   It was always ready and glad to get scientific explanations of Genesis, long before it suspected that Genesis might not be inspired truth. It pointed out with great satisfaction that the famous text of the "three witnesses" was undoubtedly spurious; and made something out of the freedom given by various readings of other famous proof-texts.   The earliest critical edition of the New Testament of very high authority — Griesbach's — was first published, I believe, in England or here, at least first circulated and studied with any zeal, by Unitarian scholars. Some of these were relieved to find that the first two chapters of Matthew do not stand on quite such firm ground as the rest, and that the narrative in Luke says nothing distinctly of a miraculous birth of Jesus; and that so, without at all denying the truth of the gospel, they might well believe (as doubtless the first Christians did) that he was the son of Joseph as well as of Mary. Some found the account of the Temptation easier to believe by supposing that the tempter was a Pharisee, or some emissary of the Jews, who wished, as it were, to feel beforehand the pulse of the new movement, or to break its force. Some found the Transfiguration best explained as an allegory or a dream.

These and other like interpretations led to the charge of playing fast and loose with the sacred narrative, and of explaining things by explaining them away. But the attempt was made in entire good faith, by men who held quite seriously to what they received as the central fact of a real revelation, and who honestly supposed they were doing good service by commending it all the better to reasonable minds. They did not see that to other minds, more positive and ardent, there are no degrees of difficulty more or less, when once they are on the supernatural plane: take it as miracle or take it as poetry, to such minds it is the exercise of the understanding itself that is offensive on such matters. The half-way rationalism of the Unitarians did the good work of training several generations in a natural, sweet, reverent, and wholesome piety; but it never has succeeded in making its own form of belief acceptable to the popular religious mind.

In the second place, it was characteristic of that movement that the interpretation it put upon doctrine was always a *moral* interpretation. Dogmatism was never allowed to dictate terms to conscience. A natural explanation was eagerly sought for the Fall of man, which was explained away into hereditary tendency, corruption of example, or infirmity of will. Election, predestination, perseverance, free grace, justification, were all reduced from the plane of dogma to that of metaphysics, and from this again to that of common-sense. Nothing was suffered to interfere with the consciousness of moral liberty, as the only ground of moral judgment of right and wrong. The atonement of human guilt by the sacrifice of an innocent being was sheer horror and blasphemy in such a view. Eternal punishment, for any sin that could be committed by a short-lived mortal, was something to be thought of with amazement and awe. The language of some passages seemed quite plain, — it might be perilous to deny it outright; but, if true, it must at any rate mean that moral guilt affects the soul itself so deeply that it can never quite recover, certainly not that that horror is arbitrarily inflicted by an inexorable God. And, as this rationalizing temper gained a little courage, it came to occupy pretty distinctly the ground of restoration in the dim future, and to bear it out with an anxious interpretation of the threatening texts.

Thus Christianity, or the doctrines of revealed religion, came to be interpreted as a system of divine

TRUTH adapted to reason and common-sense, while resting on a foundation strictly miraculous and super-natural; and as a system of human DUTY, or morality, resting on the same sanction, but wholly disengaged from metaphysical dogma. The actual duties of life were gravely, sincerely, and piously accepted, — its religious duties as well as its moral duties, whatever the enemies of the system may have supposed. I do not believe that the recognized offices of piety and worship, as well as those of honesty and charity, were ever more tenderly, seriously, and faithfully per-formed, than by the adherents of a system so unjustly represented as one of mere negation. The fervor, the passion, the stir of emotion, the warm enthusiasm that make religion a mighty power in the soul, to move whole multitudes at once, — these made no part of the Unitarian conception or experience of it. And a lack of genuine sympathy with the more popular forms of Christianity — most likely, of an adequate under-standing of them — was doubtless a great weakness in that system, as well as the source of suspicion and popular dislike.

This weakness on the emotional side was the greater pity, because under a proud and powerful Establishment, like that of England, a dissenting sect is at best in a somewhat narrowed and depressed condition; and, for its self-respect as well as its vital power, it can ill spare the strength which only reli-gious zeal or intellectual enthusiasm can give. We, whose early growth was sheltered by a modest Establishment of our own, may well honor that fear-less honesty, that sincerity of conviction, that denominational loyalty, which have been the life of English Unitarianism. It has, besides, its calendar of names which it delights to honor. And, in particular, we cannot overestimate its gain, in these later years, from the great literary and philosophical eminence, the superb ethical ideal, and the high plane of religious thought, of its best known intellectual leader, James Martineau.

But I have not set out to criticise this earlier Unitarian movement, only to state fairly what it was. It seems to me that the view now given of it — its antecedents and its characteristics — may help show how and why it came to be what it was, and make our judgment of it more intelligent and just. Without going into detail, I think we have now seen sufficiently what the doctrine really was, when first it found a recognized name and place. We know something of its strong points and its weak points ; and are prepared to understand the phases it has worn during the three periods of its history in this country, lasting something over sixty years.

II

NEW ENGLAND UNITARIANISM.

THE term Unitarian has been known in this country as the name of a religious body since the year 1815. This period, again, may be divided into three, which, for convenience, we may call the time of its Growth, including its controversy with the Orthodox sects; the time of Criticism, or of internal controversy among the parties in its own body; and the time of Construction, — that is, of scientific criticism on one hand, and of denominational organization on the other.

Each of these periods, again, is best known by the name of some representative man: the first by that of Dr. Channing; the second by that of Theodore Parker; and the third by that of Dr. Hedge, if we take it on the speculative side, or by that of Dr. Bellows, if we take it on the emotional, denominational, or constructive side. It so happens, however, that neither of these names, except the last, belongs very closely to the denomination as such. Dr. Channing never desired to be known as a Unitarian, and had a strong distrust of all denominational or sectarian names. Theodore Parker, while always asserting his right to rank with the Unitarian body, was for almost all the time of his public life in sharp and personal controversy with the great majority of its members. Dr. Hedge, probably the ablest, deepest, and most widely cultivated intellect that the denomination has embraced, is essentially a philosophical student and thinker; and, while he has given as much impulse as any man to its thought, and direction to its higher culture, he cannot be said to have done anything towards shaping those definite opinions by which a religious body is more popularly known. And it is not so much for opinion as for inspiration and organizing force that the Unitarian body is indebted to Dr. Bellows, whose splendid enthusiasm, generous range of sympathy, and magnificent working force may almost be said to have saved the denomination alive for whatever tasks may lie before it in the future.

The three dates which we may assign as the beginning of these periods are the years 1815, 1836, and 1860. No dates like these can be quite accurate as marking limits in the history of opinion. The thoughts of one generation melt into those of another like the tints of the sky after sunset. Still, each of them registers a definite fact, which may serve as well as another to start from. The first, as I said, marks the year when the Unitarian body in this country began to be known by this name, which till then had not been acknowledged or bestowed. The year 1836 may be taken, as well as any, as the birth-year of the Transcendentalism which had so much to do in shaping the form of liberal opinion we have known since; at least, for its emergence in the field of theology, for it was in that year that " the first gun of a long battle " was discharged, in a review by Mr. George Ripley of Martineau's "Rationale of Religious Inquiry," presenting views which were at once keenly and publicly attacked by Mr. Andrews Norton. The year 1860, again, dates not only the death of Theodore Parker, which brought to a close the sharpest personal controversy within the Unitarian ranks, but the moment of time when the great moral debate of our era was brought victoriously into the field of politics, and events began visibly to lead to the merging of all lesser controversies in the one absorbing struggle for the nation's life. Since then, new bearings have been taken, other issues appear, and other methods are becoming familiar in the field of speculative thought.

I shall hope to make these periods and parties more distinct in the course of the sketch which I propose to draw of the denominational life during these sixty-seven years. For it is a sketch that I propose, not a history. I shall have very little to say of events, as such; only of persons, with the opinions they represent, and the circumstances that defined their position in the religious world, whether of thought or action.

Again, I have not to do with the course of opinion in general, or the broader lines of the religious life, as would be proper if my aim were purely historical; but with a limited period, a narrow locality mostly, and a single group of persons, or series of groups, all belonging within the same general range of ideas. If this is what is meant by speaking sometimes of Unitarianism as a "family affair" and a "Boston notion," I shall for the present admit the charge, at least not question it. Unitarianism is, in fact, to a great extent a local growth : it has had but little of a temper of propagandism, and a rather scanty denominational history. I have sometimes thought that its real comfort and pride in former days, to speak it honestly, were in its narrow range, its family likeness, its absence of sectarian activity or ambition. There is next to nothing to tell of enterprise and adventure ; or rather, while there have been noble individual examples, there has been comparatively little of concerted, well-planned denominational action.

The denomination — that is, the men composing it — have never been stingy ; none less so. It would be within bounds to say that their gifts for religious, charitable, and other public objects (especially educational), outside their very liberal scale of church expenses, could be reckoned by a good many millions of dollars in these last fifty years. By far the largest part of this has been put quietly out of sight in colleges, in theological instruction or publications, in home missions and works of charity, in remote churches, and so on, and has never made a figure in denominational reports. In fact, there has been a great shyness, a very unnecessary modesty and reticence, if not a positive dislike, among some of the most generous Unitarians, of anything that looked like sectarian glory : Mr. Amos Lawrence, for example, one of the most intelligent and liberal of merchants, gave, it is said, to orthodox institutions twice over what he did within the lines of his own denominational connection. This peculiarity, if not eccentricity of character, has to be taken into account, in summing up the position of Unitarianism in America, and in making any estimate of it as a working force.

There is another point as to which one should speak with some reserve, which yet is really necessary to be taken into account in our review. It is implied in what I have already said of the Unitarian body being represented by a group of men quite independent of one another as thinkers, but standing personally in very near relations together. I should desire in this view to bring you, if I could, one step nearer to this group, nearer to a personal interest in the men who made it, and to a personal acquaintance with them. This is the more necessary, because Unitarian opinion has always been an individual thing. No one ever claimed to speak as responsible for the thoughts of other men, or as holding them responsible for his. Nothing, in fact, except a personal acquaintance which goes behind the spoken or published word, entitles one to speak with any confidence of the position of individuals in a group of men so entirely independent of one another, — independent, I mean, as to opinion; independent, except it be in the way of a common sympathy and culture, and a mutual good-will and respect.

This I may do with the more confidence here, because the lifetime of the denomination itself is easily embraced in the memory of many of its older members, and is not many years longer than my own. As a child I was brought up in the midst of all its influences, within hearing of all its earlier controversies, and with a child's natural interest and pride in the names which were considered then to do it honor;

while my earlier university and professional life was just when the controversies of the second period began to take shape and force, bringing me into relations more or less close with most of the men who gave its particular stamp and coloring to the movement which I am trying to interpret.

I will recall here — not going outside the lines of that personal acquaintance just referred to — a few of these representative names. There was the venerable Aaron Bancroft, father of the historian, and pioneer of liberal theology in central Massachusetts; Dr. Channing, who for more than thirty years was more closely identified than any other with the denominational thought and life; the Henry Wares, father and son, who were both in a very special sense associated with the foundation and earlier history of this School; George Putnam, their kinsman by marriage, long the most brilliant and admired preacher of the Boston circle, — whose clear argumentative statement commanded the respect of trained lawyers, — whose large sense matched the worldly wisdom of merchant and financier, — the eloquent orator of homely morality and the religion of every-day life, which his touch transfigured to poetry and splendor; Orville Dewey, in whom thought is more intimately blended with emotion than in any other I can recall, — whom I have heard Dr. Putnam call the greatest preacher that probably ever had been or would be, — who seemed to make the pulpit a confessional, — whose large and brooding intellect set itself to interpret the deeper experience of the Christian life, — whose mind was generously open, till long past eighty, to the lat-

est methods or discoveries in the pursuit of truth;
President Walker, whose shrewd wisdom, generous
tolerance, wide philosophic culture, and dignity of
character were not more remarkable than the cordial
and kindly sympathy he always had for younger
men; those three most eminent theological scholars
of their day, Norton, Palfrey, and Noyes, whose best
work was given to theological education here; John
Pierpont, tender religious poet and high-tempered
pulpit warrior, proud, irascible, always eagerly pressing home some sharp point of his generous and hot
conviction; Ephraim Peabody, the beloved minister
of King's Chapel, whose face was a benediction, — in
whom gravity, sweetness, and a cautious wisdom
were blended in a combination as rare as it was
lovely; Theodore Parker, the generous, dauntless, in-
corrigible apostle of free thought, the heroic leader in
social and political reform, pioneer of the many who
in these latter years have forsaken the ancient ways;
Ezra Stiles Gannett, the eloquent and noble colleague
of Channing, most fervent and devoted of men, whose
conscience, morbidly acute, was burdened with every
grief and sin of the city where he did his work, —
whose burning speech almost inspired the cool temper
of Boston Unitarianism with his own missionary zeal,
— of whom it may well be said that ten such men
would have carried Unitarianism like a prairie fire
from border to border of our country; Thomas Starr
King, that bright electric light of liberal theology,
whose flame went out, alas! on the Pacific coast
eighteen years ago, — whose memory is wonderfully
fresh and near to any who knew him, as the most

genial of friends, the most cheerful and instructive of companions, the most lucid, swift, and radiant intelligence that it has ever been our joy to know.

To these I should add a few names of eminent laymen best known to the general public, and variously representing the Unitarian fellowship and idea : John Quincy Adams, notably the one most thoroughbred statesman that our country has produced, put in office by Washington in early manhood, an eloquent lecturer in this University, experienced in diplomacy at several European courts, and after his presidency the veteran champion of the national honor in the House of Representatives ; his cousin Judge Cranch, the noble, upright, sweet-hearted, and devout Chief-Justice of the District of Columbia for more than forty years ; President Quincy, last of the proud old Boston Federalists, who died at the age of ninety-three, the most honored citizen of New England ; Chief-Justice Shaw, one of the most learned of American jurists, and solidest in judgment on the bench, which he dignified for nearly thirty years ; Edward Everett, the most cultivated intellect, probably, that has ever taken part in our national counsels ; Charles Sumner, chivalrous and fearless champion of the Higher Law in the darkest crisis of our history; Governor Andrew, who more than any other man carried the heart of New England with him through the war; Ralph Waldo Emerson, too, in early life a Unitarian preacher, now everywhere recognized as first in the highest department of our native literature, so lately gone that it is as if he were still among us, serene, eloquent, beloved, in the sphere he made and bright-

ened by his radiance; these, with Bryant and Long-
fellow, and a host of other names that have adorned
the literature of our country, belong to the history of
New England Unitarianism, and ought not to be
spared from the briefest record that attempts to trace
its character.

When each of the names here noted recalls a distinct personal reminiscence, and most of them a personal relation more or less intimate and dear, you
will not wonder that I find it difficult to say, out of
hand, just what the Unitarian opinion is on any
given matter, or what it is that Unitarians believe
in general; or that I am a little impatient that they
should ever be judged by their theology, which was
so small a fraction of either their religion or their
life !

Such men as most of those here named could not
be — I may say, could not afford to be — dogmatists,
enthusiasts, sectarians, propagandists of their own
opinions. As for us others, it is simply a privilege
and honor to count as the most obscure and undis-
tinguished in such a company. Unitarians have not
been united by fidelity to any creed, but by sharing,
each in his own way, a common spirit and life. For
myself, I have spoken to more than a hundred and
fifty of their congregations, and have met groups or
families of their communion in numerous other places,
from Hungary to Oregon, everywhere and always
finding myself equally at home. And thus the phrase
" common spirit and life " has a very distinct meaning
to my mind, quite different from what it would be if
I only copied it out of a book.

I have said that the Unitarian body in this country, either in its origin or in its history, was not a Sect in the common understanding of that term. It has had no creed, no platform, no policy, as a sect; and it is only of late, and rather feebly, that it has made any effort to propagate itself aggressively within the lines of other sects and creeds.

When I speak of sects in this connection, I do not mean so much those bodies which had a recognized historical existence before the settlement of this country, and made part of its original religious or even political organization, — such as the Congregationalists, the Presbyterians, the Episcopalians, and (as in this list I think I ought to include) the Methodists. These are simply forms of church government or organization, and may consist with any laxity of opinion. Thus the main body of American Unitarians are Congregational; those in England are or were Presbyterian; the first church in Boston to declare itself unitarian was Episcopal, and remains so in its forms of worship; and preachers have continued in the Methodist connection with avowed unitarian opinions, with the full understanding and by the strong urgency of their brethren.

All these, if I understand the matter rightly, dealt originally with *the whole population as such,* in the places where they were respectively established, and were not special or outside organizations, made up of those of a peculiar way of thinking. Among these last, or sects proper, I should especially rank the large, vigorous, strong, and aggressive bodies of the Baptists and Universalists, which are founded each upon an idea. Their organization, their policy, their definite and aggressive creed, but in particular their secession from other religious bodies in the name of that creed, are what makes them Sects, as distinct from the more general term religious body, church, or communion. Now the Unitarians do not belong to the former class, because their opinions distinctly exclude them. They do not belong to the latter class, because they have no distinct creed or policy of their own. Yet again, as claiming a church polity, or communion, and a recognized fellowship of their own, they are quite as far removed from the ranks, or rather from the scattered individualisms, of "free inquirers" or "free religionists," with whom they would hold it the most glaring misunderstanding to be confounded.

I have tried to say what the Unitarian body is not. The question next comes, What is it?

To this the answer has been made, that it is like one of those unincorporated districts of land which are sometimes left out when the boundaries of towns and villages have been marked out all round them.[1] The soil may be as good, the farms may yield as large an increase, the families may be as contented, prosperous, and happy; but they do not belong to any known political organization.

That comparison will go a little way: it expresses the fact of independence, but it does not express the fact of unity. It leaves the look of the matter as if Unitarian churches were only chance and random gatherings, nuclei as it were of religious organization

[1] The comparison was made, very felicitously, by Dr. Putnam.

and effort, in that large vague half of the community which is sometimes lumped together as "unchurched." Now this means too little, and it means too much. It means too much, because it turns our thought upon that wide chaos of opinion, incoherent and unformed, which, as "independent" or as "unchurched," already occupies full half our field of vision when we look that way, and which is constantly enlarged by the shelling off or the undermining of elements which are not well compacted among our twenty or more religious bodies.   It means too little, because it overlooks the one thing which gives a consistency and unity to this particular body, and makes it possible to gather its statistics, and in some degree to direct its corporate action.

That one thing is the first thing of all which should be made clear, if we would know either the history, the character, or the present attitude of Unitarianism.   It is that, historically, *it is the liberal wing of the great Congregational body* which founded the first colonies in New England, and gave the law to Church and State for more than two hundred years. Of a list of three hundred and sixty-six Unitarian churches, one hundred and twenty or more (including a large majority of those in Massachusetts) were original local parishes formed under the first ecclesiastical polity of the Puritan Congregationalists.[1] Of these, again, thirty-eight were founded before the year 1700, including that first organized by the refugees in Leyden in 1620, a few months before the colony landed on Plymouth Rock; and eighty more — that is, one

[1] See " Year Book of the Unitarian Congregational Churches."

hundred and eighteen in all, or more than one third of the entire number — were established before the war of the Revolution. Thus the church history of Unitarianism in this country runs back almost to the time of the colony at Jamestown, and about two hundred years before the name Unitarian was either given to or accepted by one of its congregations. I do not say the expression of unitarian opinion; but the corporate history and the ecclesiastical traditions belong to the Congregational body at large, and not to that of a separate and peculiar sect. That is to say, again, that Unitarianism has received its full share of the original inheritance of that great Puritan body which made the English Commonwealth and the Pilgrim Colonies of America.

I say this not at all to enter a claim which some persons might be unwilling to allow, but simply to state the historical fact of the case. This one fact more than any other explains the nature and the seeming inconsistency of the Unitarian record. That is, while Unitarians have been mostly known for their liberal opinion, for their defence of free inquiry, and for their tolerance of out-and-out scientific or philosophical radicalism, — at the same time the temper of the body at large has been mainly conservative. The large majority of Unitarians, truth to say, have been extremely annoyed and scandalized by the results to which younger, more restless, more bold and positive minds have been led; while these, again, have been full of angry wonder and reproach that any limits at all should be set to that free speculation and inquiry to which they felt themselves invited.

The misunderstanding was inevitable.   By their history and antecedents Unitarians make as ancient and conservative a religious body as any in this country.   They adopted, however, very early, liberal principles of interpretation; and these, after the unpleasant shock of "radicalism" has been got well over, will no doubt result in a serious, scholarly, scientific, as well as independent criticism, noway hostile to the organic religious life.

The real origin, then, of the Unitarian body in this country was, that a large proportion of the Congregational body in eastern Massachusetts, including all the leading churches in Boston but one, had come, from sixty to eighty years ago, gradually to adopt liberal opinions — at first Arminian (or free-will) as opposed to Calvinistic, and afterwards Unitarian as opposed to Trinitarian.[1]   Just how and why this division of opinion had come about, it is not easy to say.   It corresponds nearly enough with the natural division we always find among people of the same general way of thinking, some rigid and strict, some loose or liberal.   In particular, it seemed to grow from the influence, and to follow the widening circle of culture, that went out from Harvard College, —

[1] I think this was the case in every country town of large population in eastern Massachusetts except three, — Charlestown, Andover, and Ipswich, which were kept from following the drift of liberal opinion by the personal weight and influence of their preachers: at least this is true of the able and rigid Dr. Morse of Charlestown.   This drift of liberal opinion reached back about forty miles, its northerly half then extending westward as far as the Connecticut River, and lapping over into southern New Hampshire. These limits, adding a few of the larger coast-towns, define pretty nearly the geographical extent of New England Unitarianism.

then as now a chief centre of secular learning in this country. The men who were most moved by this influence, or who were in advance of it, were often called — by a phrase borrowed, I believe, from Robert Boyle — the "Latitude-men about Cambridge." The free-thinking of the Revolutionary period may have had something to do, but I should think not much, with this latitude of opinion.

The circumstance which more than any other brought it into public notice and recognition was the appointment of Henry Ware to the post of professor of Divinity in Harvard College, in 1805. This was strongly protested against at the time by the more orthodox party, as bad faith to the founder of that professorship, — the eminent and generous London puritan, Thomas Hollis; and it is deplored to this day, with indignant grief, by that party, who do not abandon their hope of seeing the University brought back to the faith of the fathers.

This personal episode helps to explain a good deal of the sharp tone in the controversy that followed. Still there was no breach in the Congregational ranks for ten years after, nor a very open one for some years later still. The forward steps that led to forming a Unitarian party were in the way of literary and scholarly criticism. It happened that a very brilliant group of young men — cultivated, ardent, eloquent — graduated from the University in those days, of whom Edward Everett became best known to history; but Joseph Stevens Buckminster — a preacher in Boston for some five years, until his death in 1812 — had far the strongest influence, by the singular grace of his oratory, his wonderful social charm, his eager and diligent enthusiasm as a scholar. Forty years after his death, I have heard it told, there were Boston merchants who could not speak of him without tears. This bright circle of personal force and culture was organized in the then famous "Anthology Club," which started one of the first literary and critical journals of the country, the "Monthly Anthology,"— lineal predecessor of the "Christian Disciple," "Christian Examiner," and "Unitarian Review,"— which was really the harbinger and mouthpiece of early Unitarian theology.

I shall not trouble you with any account of the controversy which followed. It is admirably told by Mr. William Gannett in his father's Biography, and need not be told again. The details of battles and skirmishes of opinion are apt to be a very dull part of the history of any time, except where some strong personal interest comes in. I wish, however, to illustrate from another point of view the nature of the change which was going on; and this I shall find it easiest to do by a single example.

As you know, by ecclesiastical law the Congregational Order made part of the original constitution of New England. Each town must maintain a church or parish organization, and every voter must be a church-member. This old constitution of things was not wholly done away in Massachusetts till 1833, when the Voluntary system was fully adopted. Till then, every citizen's tax-bill included a religious tax; and, till 1820, that tax must be paid for the support of a Congregational Church.

For example, my father was settled in 1816 as
minister of a country town. The settlement was for
life, and the salary was directly voted and paid by
the Town from the same fund that made the town
roads, supported the town schools, and paid for the
petty town police of constable, fence-viewer, and
local surveyor. Quite within my own recollection,
his ordinary household expenses were paid by drafts
on the town treasurer, exactly as they would be by
cheques upon a bank. One rigid old-school puritan,
Asaph Rice, had opposed and dissented from my
father's settlement on the ground of his liberal theology; and probably the majority would have been
quite as well satisfied with a more orthodox preacher;
but that did not prevent them all, Asaph Rice included, from being good friends and contented parish-
ioners. Nor did the same thing prevent, for a while
at least, the common professional courtesies in neigh-
boring towns, from orthodox and liberal alike. Sectarian lines, since so sharply marked and so jealously
guarded, were only beginning to be known. The
charming simplicity of this arrangement only began
to be disturbed in 1827 by the formation in the vil-
lage of a little Baptist church, which was a great grief
to my father, since the first steps in it were taken by
near personal friends of his, who were conscientious
enough to tax themselves at the start the extra cost
of it, after paying their share to the support of the
legal Parish. This, of course, they felt to be a great
injustice,—as in fact it was; and in six years more
that hardship was removed by the law of complete
ecclesiastical freedom, under which we are now living.

Now a legal establishment can never be a sect, properly speaking. It has got to meet not only the average mind, but a great variety of minds. It must include a wide latitude of opinion, and admit considerable freedom of debate. It may be fairly doubted whether the conditions of a general, manly, healthy, liberal, charitable growth of religious thought are ever so well met as in the breadth, the decency, the broad tolerance of a religious establishment, when sustained with general consent by a serious and intelligent population. Very great religious earnestness it does not admit, at least it does not favor. The "great awakening" under Jonathan Edwards was a solitary phenomenon (which in fact banished him from his Northampton parish), and the "revival" under Whitefield was by a force from abroad. Both, it may fairly be assumed, led to a reaction in the direction of liberalism, which they helped full as much as they opposed. The sober common-sense view of religion, which makes it in the broadest way religion for the people, is nourished nowhere so well, I think, as in an establishment like that of a century ago in New England, which sheltered the growth of manly liberal unsectarian thought, which nurtured a generous and growing scholarship, and which has left its mark on nothing more deep and distinct than on the entire Unitarian movement in this country, so far as it can be traced to that source.

In conclusion, I will speak very briefly of that movement at the period when it still retained most distinctly the features of its origin, and was represented by that group of strong and excellent men whom I have spoken of before. This period may be taken, roughly, as from forty to fifty years ago.

The general theory of Christianity as accepted at this stage, which is sometimes called "old-school Unitarianism," was (as President Walker was in the habit of describing it) especially adapted to the mind, shaped as it were to the demand, not of speculative theologians, but of serious and educated laymen. Such representative names as those of Judge White, Judge Story, and Judge Shaw at once occur, when we recall that period. These men clung to Christianity with the tenacious hold of an honest reverence and a strong conviction; with a trained masculine understanding, also, which tolerated no affront to reason or good morals. Paley and Lardner had established the historical foundations: the structure to be built upon them was that of rational piety, personal morality, and civic virtue. This was the manly, dignified, and sober type of "Boston Unitarianism," a name never to be named without gratitude and honor.

Lawyer-like, too, it was impatient, perhaps intolerant, of any questioning of the foundations. The Bible, these men held, was a minister's credentials. Make what abatement in the popular notion of it you may and must: then take it, or else leave it, for what it claims to be, — a revelation of absolute authority to declare the law of life, or to instruct the mind on the highest conceivable truth. To their strong and sober sense, Christianity, without a supernatural revelation of truth, without miracles, without the divine authority of Jesus, was a weak delusion, if not a

wicked and hypocritical pretence. The subtilties of
theologians, the refinements of criticism, were not for
their style of mind. Christianity was holy and venerable to them, because it meant that virtue which
regulates the life and saves the State. In the words
which I copy from the clear firm autograph of President Quincy, — the accurate and perfect expression
of this mental temper, — "Human happiness has no
perfect security but freedom; freedom none but virtue;
virtue none but knowledge: and neither freedom, virtue, nor knowledge has any vigor or immortal hope,
except in the principles of the Christian faith, and in
the sanctions of the Christian religion."

I wish to express, with all the emphasis of which
I am capable, my veneration and gratitude for these
noble men, and for the type of rational, manly, and
tender piety which they have left us. I will not insult their memory by a single word of apology ; by
arguing whether they, or those who have endeavored
to follow their lead, are to be vouchsafed the honor
of the Christian name. Small honor to that name, if
they disclaim it or are deprived of it!

There are two sorts of people who do them and the
movement they represent a great injustice : those in
other sects or at a distance, who fancy something in
it cold, haughty, and exclusive ; and the liberals of a
younger day, who think with a certain lofty disdain
of its strict and austere conservatism. But to those
of my own generation the life that was in its veins
gave the very mother's milk on which we were nurtured ; and it is impossible to think of it without a
certain filial tenderness. Nay, such is the force of

reverent habit, I am apt to think that Christianity, in all its ages of evolution, and in all its numberless forms, has never taken a type at once so free from ecclesiastical pressure, and in itself so manly, sweet, and noble. A faith which expressed itself in the ideal thought of Channing, the Consolations and Hymns of Greenwood, the tender wisdom of Ephraim Peabody; a personal piety whose profession and aim were the "Formation of the Christian Character;" a charity which created the Fraternity of Churches, and has made itself felt for fifty years in the tone and pattern of every good work done in that community, — these may very well challenge comparison with anything its critics have to show; and may very well make those of us who think we have outgrown it pause to consider whether, for a generation or two at any rate, we are likely to find anything so good to take its place.

III.

CHANNING.

IT was the great felicity of Unitarianism in this country to be represented for twenty-five years by the pure and eminent name of William Ellery Channing. If anything could possibly disarm the hostility of sectarian prejudice, if anything could possibly enlist the affectionate pride and loyalty of the body of which he was the acknowledged head, it would be the elevated plane of thought, the fervent yet passionless eloquence, the sweet and tender piety, the transparent purity of conscience braced in later life to an intrepid vigor, the single-minded devotion to the highest order of truth, of this great religious leader.

I use these words with careful deliberation. I have not myself always felt in fact, as I appreciate now in deliberate review, his real intellectual eminence. The bolder temper, the deeper learning, the scientific habit, the intenser political passion, the restless speculation, of the period that has passed since his death, all serve to hide from us the grandeur of the work he did, and its indispensable service in educating the very best qualities of mind and soul, on which we have to rely for the work most needed in the future.

For his own personality was not aggressive and commanding, as that of most other men of equal eminence. It was by persuasion and not impression — by pressure (as Dr. Bellows once finely said of him) and not by blows — that he made his deep mark on his own generation and on ours. Each single quality of an intellectual leader, taken by itself, might seem to be wanting in him. In all his writings it would be hard to find a daring thought or a brilliant phrase. His own small communion has produced or included much more learned scholars, men of much deeper and broader speculative grasp, preachers of far greater brilliancy, fervor, fancy, eloquence, and popular pulpit power, bolder and more radical thinkers in the direction either of scientific criticism or moral reform. Of the many eminent names belonging, by nature or adoption, to the Unitarian pulpit of New England, several have made their mark in some one direction, and perhaps more, sharper and deeper than Channing did, but none of them near so broadly. None of them would be once thought of — with the single exception of Theodore Parker — as having left the distinct impression of his mind upon a religious or intellectual movement, to which he had given tone and character; none of them, with that exception, would be once thought of as the recognized and unchallenged chief of such a movement.

That distinction is allowed, in our religious history, unquestioned and ungrudged, to Channing alone. And, as I said, I think it is justified by the most critical and deliberate judgment of the case. But to make it appear just to those who were strangers to the movement, in the absence of almost all those salient points which most easily catch the distant eye, it is necessary to consider with some attention the man himself, and the circumstances of his time.

The life of Dr. Channing extends just over sixty-two years, from 1780 to 1842. His childhood was spent at Newport, Rhode Island, where his mind received a very serious bent from that eccentric, stern, and godly old Calvinist, Dr. Hopkins, — whose name is best known from his famous tenet, that the true test of fitness to be saved is willingness to be damned for the glory of God. By that extraordinary tenet the name "Hopkinsian" has been conserved in sectarian tradition to this day. The boy Channing was little of person, gentle and serious of temper; yet one story is told, to his credit, of a time when that gentle temper flamed out into wrath, and into something of a school-boy fight, I believe, in defence of some younger comrade. No one who saw him in manhood would suspect that he had ever been capable of wrath. That one flash of it was a symptom of moral health.

His walks by the beach, and the fresh wind and rolling surge of the Atlantic, did a good deal, he says, to nurture a certain dreamy and devout sympathy with nature: his spiritual horizon, all through his life, kept always that level width. Excepting this, and a native sensitiveness of organization almost feminine, there was little to distinguish him at twenty — little, that is, of native genius or intellectual force — from a goodly number of serious, generous, and cultivated young men who graduate year by year from our American colleges. With him it was, with them it is, a pure, high, consecrated aim.

His first larger experience of life was had in Richmond, Virginia, where, I imagine, his position as teacher helped to seclude him from any wide range of social intercourse, as well as his own temper of mind, and his moral repugnance to the state of society there, which came out long afterwards in his hostility to slavery. But, in particular, it was in the solitary reflection of these years that he quite outgrew, and firmly renounced, the narrow creed of his youth, — or what there was narrow in it, — and found himself, intelligently and consistently, in the ranks of liberal thinkers.

I should say, however, that the process with him was not one of criticism, hardly of investigation, but an even, natural, and very devout religious growth. Every step of it was taken, not merely with anxious deliberation, but with a certain tender, solicitous, remorseful, conscientious, pleading piety and religious discipline of soul, which make the record of those years like the record of old saints and pietists. The prospect was rather that of a morbid introspective pietism, than of a manly, courageous, cheerful, and healthy religious life, which it afterwards so largely became.

To this somewhat hectic experience and temper of that time we have to add a great loss of bodily health and vigor from the exposures of his sea-voyage home. Physically he was never a robust man, never, I should suppose, well in health, after those years of his stay in Richmond. His stature was small, his frame attenuated, his face thin. The clear wide brow, the great, solemn, wistful eyes, the low, melodious, and flowing speech, — these were native gifts potent to win through a strong and sweet persuasion; but they were united in him with a physical frailty that might seem to forbid the hope of any serious life-work, and with a bodily frame that seemed but enough (to cite again the words of Dr. Bellows) to anchor his soul to the earth.

He was never quite an invalid, but he was always a valetudinarian. In particular, he had a singular sensitiveness to cold; and the recollection of many of his friends will recall his presence, oftenest, at the fireside corner of his warmly sheltered and softly furnished room. That soft and warm shelter he seemed always to crave and need as much as a sick child. What to a more vigorous man would be indolent indulgence, with him was a necessity of life and the condition of any working force. Circumstances gave him, through all his working and declining years, this necessary shelter, and screened him from the raw wind of the world by the surroundings and the comforts of sufficient wealth. His virtue lay not in manly struggle with difficulty and hardship, but in the consecration of life-long leisure and ample opportunity to something very different from a selfish luxury. He had as little of the storm and battle of life as can fall to any serious man to encounter; but was surrounded always by the respectful, affectionate, vigilant, and almost too obsequious homage and love of near friends. Ideally, his thought took in the

widest sweep of duty and every sacred sympathy
and homely obligation that bind man to his kind:
personally, he was perplexed, shrinking, helpless, in
the presence of any one of the rougher tasks that
would bring him face to face with coarse suffering
and want. The sensitive, womanly temperament,
with the self-consideration that in an invalid becomes
the necessary instinct of self-defence, made some persons quick and harsh to judge what seemed to cross
his own serious pleadings and maxims of self-denial;
but no person was ever brought very near to him,
who went for sympathy or counsel, or in simple
friendship, that did not bear the same testimony to
the infinite sweetness, elevation, serenity, the absolute freedom from personal passion and desire, which
were the root of his extraordinary moral power.

For a very genuine and great moral power this
tenderly nurtured mind became, and is felt to this
day — warm, life-generating, springlike — among all
the more turbulent forces that play upon the world.
The process, too, by which it grew to this great spiritual predominance and power was as gentle and patient
as the spring growth in which its buds began to
swell. Somewhere about the age of thirty his name
began to win upon the public ear as a preacher of
singular fervor and beauty of utterance, along with
the more brilliant reputation of Buckminster, then at
its height. It is not easy to describe, though it is
perhaps not very difficult to imagine, the manner and
gifts that won their way so surely. In his own place
in the Federal Street pulpit I heard him only once,
and saw him only once or twice besides, — barely

enough to verify the impression which others have recorded. From the stilted and awkward height of that old-fashioned lofty mahogany pulpit, with its tall balustraded flights of stairs, his face beamed down, it might be said without exaggeration, like the face of an angel, and his voice floated down like a voice from higher spheres. I cannot think of any other preacher of those who can fairly be called popular, to whom that distant altitude, so lifting him away from his congregation, might be called even a positive help, as it seemed to be with him.

Dr. Channing's voice, again, was of rare power and attraction, — clear, melodious, flowing, slightly plaintive, so as curiously to catch and win upon the hearer's sympathy: its melody and pathos in the reading of a hymn were alone a charm that might bring men to the listening, like the attraction of sweet music. Often, too, when the signs of physical frailty were apparent, it might be said that his speech was watched and waited for with that sort of hush, as if one were waiting to catch his last earthly words. All the strength that was in the man went out from him in pure spiritual fervor and uplifting moral force. Any speech that could be called eloquent, or any eloquence that could be called popular, could not possibly have depended less than his on what are commonly regarded as oratorical gifts; could not possibly have consisted more than his in the qualities which make a pure, disembodied, spiritual radiance.

It follows directly from this, that that power could not have been felt, at least could not have been developed, in a resisting medium. It was the great felicity of Dr. Channing's experience, that early in life he found his place in a sphere which offered no hindrance, but rather invited out and welcomed just those qualities in which he was afterwards so distinguished. His people included what was very best of the serious, devout, conscientious, liberal-minded who made the finest type of early Unitarianism. As a sculptor would wish to work in marble of the purest waxen lustre, as a musician would wish to compose for instruments of the finest tone, so there were men and women in that company whom it would be such a preacher's highest joy and privilege to win towards the higher life. A spirit " is not finely touched but to fine issues." The inspiring, sympathetic touch may come first from the speaker, but it must go back to him from the hearer, warm and quick, before the speaker can become an *orator*, — which word means, not a declaimer, but one who *pleads* with power and effect. Such effective pleading, on the plane of high, pure, passionless, spiritual truth, made the rare pulpit power of Dr. Channing; and it was a power which largely grew from the harmony which he found, or made, in the atmosphere of the place where his voice was heard.

It may be reckoned ten years of professional life before his name began to be known publicly as a leader in religious thought; and again fifteen more, before it began to be heard in a wider sphere, — as it was for about ten years, — in the discussion of the gravest questions of morals and politics. So that his professional life has three stages, — as preacher, as theologian, and as reformer.

It is no part of my purpose to criticise or dicusss the work of these three periods. That of the first, in particular, would probably be found to be the treatment of the ordinary pulpit topics, — the nurture of Christian piety, and the religious discipline of life, — distinguished from other men's rather by tone than substance. The work of the later periods belongs in large part to the general history of religious thought or denominational annals, and to that of the broader moral movements of the day, — education, peace, temperance, and antislavery. To turn rapidly the pages of that noble half-century volume in which his discussions of those matters are gathered, along with the earlier fruitage of his life, would give a fairer view than any critical summing up of the range and measure of his power. There is, however, a view to be taken of his work which is quite necessary to understand the peculiar place it holds in our religious development, and especially to show how it connects itself with what went before and after in the particular movement of thought to which that work belonged.

Of his gifts purely personal I have spoken, perhaps enough, already. But there are two things, besides, that are very characteristic of his mind, and that in their combination seem best to define the nature of the movement of which he was so eminent a leader.

The first was *a very keen and almost morbid sense of moral evil.* This "conviction of sin" was quite as genuine a fruit as any from the stern old Calvinistic stock out of which his own faith grew. It differed however in him, very widely, from the two forms in which it is most commonly found, and which are appealed to by religionists generally with most emphasis and effect.

That sort of conversion, or religious crisis, of which Augustine's is the most famous and Bunyan's the most familiar type, could never have been the experience of Channing. It was when he was still a child that he quite outgrew, on one side at least, his liability to that great shock and catastrophe of religious fear. He had heard a sermon on the terrors of the Lord, which to his childish mind seemed to wrap life all around, and the bright world itself, in gloom and dread: surely, he thought, if this is true, none of us can ever smile again. But his father, who was a serious man, seemed to feel none of this alarm, and his cheerful unconcern, with his excellent appetite at dinner, gave the boy at first a shock like jesting at a funeral; but soon convinced him, once for all, that the whole thing was unreal and untrue. The grave sense of evil, the real "conviction of sin," was not diminished; but, happily for that clear conscience and sensitive organization, it never lay, to his thought, against that lurid background of a universe of horror.

It was impossible, too, that his dreamy, meditative boyhood, the simple purity of his country life, the high and devout temper of thought so early trained, should ever be made the groundwork of the keen self-reproach, the passionate remorse, the agonized inward struggle, which with so many men of saintly virtue have been the narrow gateway of the higher life. It must have been a calm ascent, and not a sharp con-

flict against spiritual foes that beset the climbing.
That life was from the first a process, a culture, a
growth, — not a warfare, a fight, a victory. At least,
though every step in advance is in some sense a
conquest over something, the impression he kept of
it, and the lesson he would always enforce, was of a
method calm, even, and natural. I do not remember
that he hints anywhere at a knowledge or an understanding of spiritual conflict, such as one would
have to whom that conflict had been very real.
Whatever lack of intensity, of the deeper springs of
moral power, has been found in his life or writings
makes them so much the more genuine expression
of a religious nurture singularly passionless and calm,
and so the more characteristic of his special method
and power.

And, again, that conviction of sin was not intensi-
fied, as it is with many, by the spectacle of the grosser
wrongs or sufferings among men. His experience of
life was in the main placid, secluded, uneventful. It
is a wholesome contrast if we think of it in connection with the stern Calvinism inflicted on the gentle
and sensitive temper of the poet Cowper by John
Newton, whose earlier life had been spent as master
of a slave-ship. Of slavery, with some of its sorrows and wrongs, Channing did get a nearer view in
St. Croix ; and these lay always close and heavy
upon his conscience. But even these — and, much
more, the inhumanities of street, factory, mine, hos-
pital, or prison — lay in his mind not so much as
vivid pictures of wrong inflicted and suffering endured, but rather as the shadow, intense and deep in

quality but very dim in outline, which darkened his broad and generous idealizings of human life.

He saw the particular fact, when his mind dwelt upon it at all, in its broad relations. The right thing was a spot of color, and the wrong thing a spot of gloom, in a wide landscape, which he looked at somewhat vaguely (as one might if a little near-sighted), more with a poet's emotion than with an artist's eye. That keen and troubled sense of a deep reality in what human life displays of evil was al-ways with him, — if nothing more, at least as a dim background to relieve his far more vivid conception of spiritual truth and right. But the action of his imagination upon the facts and forms that made up the picture was brooding and slow. So far as it af-fected his appeals and efforts in behalf of goodness, it was more in a vague, general way, to deepen the tone, quicken the motive, and give distinct sense of elevation to the religious life, than to intensify it by the passion and the dread of sin. So that here, too, a certain breadth and placidity, rather than vehe-mence and depth, mark the quality of his power.

It is only against some opposing evil that any form of goodness can be felt, as motive or as fact. It is only as violation of the highest good our minds can know, that we really feel the dread and power of wrong. The Calvinistic scheme, which Channing was taught in his youth, gave a very keen sense of sin, in the soul or in the world, as enmity and rebel-lion against the sovereignty of God. To us that phrase has become a figure of speech, — a symbol, covering a relation of right and wrong which we can see better, or think we can, under a different sort of symbol.

The religious terror, almost we might even say the religious awe, before God as sovereign and judge, has greatly faded from the mind of a generation trained to think of him as Father rather than Sovereign, as Comforter rather than Judge. Some other opposite must be conceived, over against the passions, temptations, and wrongs of life; or else our religious theory slides towards a futile Optimism on the one hand, or a gloomy Fatalism on the other. Our moral sense craves some point of resistance and relief. The majesty of Goodness may not be as "awful" to our thought as it was to Milton's, who makes the King of Darkness quail before it, — though only for a moment. But at least that majesty must be something real, something that can be set in contrast over against our human degradation, guilt, and pain. This upward look, this necessary contrast, this sustaining force, Channing found in his favorite doctrine of *the dignity of human nature*. This topic more than any other made the burden of his preaching, and the central point, from which he reached out towards the Right he upheld on one side, or the Wrong he attacked on the other.

It is to be observed that this idealizing view of his, this profound, lively, and sacred sense of the dignity of human nature, is quite as much opposed to the view which pessimists and cynics have made painfully familiar in our day, as it is to the austere and dreadful conviction of the divine judgments, which marked the theology of a former time. This new gospel of Humanity — remote alike from religious terror and irreligious contempt — made the very special burden of Channing's message to his generation. The dignity of human nature he elevated into a religious dogma, as with himself it was an inspiration and a creed. How far it consisted with the facts of human nature was no more his care, than how far the facts of human life consist with the moral providence of God. "So much the worse for the facts." At any rate, those facts were screened from his eye — at least, greatly softened and dimmed in outline — by the peculiar seclusion which sheltered while it developed his religious life.

The growth was healthy, not morbid; vigorous, if not robust, — whether by virtue or in spite of that still seclusion. What I have called the "gospel of humanity," announced in the pure tone and with the earnest conviction native to him, made, more than any other word that has been spoken to this century, the religious creed of the finest, broadest, deepest minds. It retained from the first dispensation of Christianity all its fervor, its purity, its sweetness; it caught from modern life its instinct of justice, its wider social sympathies, its warm and lively hope of a coming victory of natural and inalienable right.

Above all, where the contrast shows strongest against the earlier creed, it was a *generous* faith. It was full of a noble confidence in man's nature and destiny, full of a noble sympathy with what is best in all forms of natural goodness, full of a noble aspiration towards a better earthly future for man and the redress of all evils in society, as well as the victories of conscience in the soul. And it was a form of modern piety all the more strongly marked in him, because relieved against that earnest and sincere, but dreadful and implacable, belief from which the religious experience of his early years had set him free.

The thought has been made quite too familiar to us, as part of the peculiar gospel of our time, to need dwelling on here. But it may be worth while to notice, very briefly, how from this central position Dr. Channing met and did those tasks which have made his name best known, and given it the widest influence.

There are, first, three or four discourses of Doctrine, —the same which made him the unchallenged and even revered leader of his own religious body. The event which more than any other gave them the courage of their convictions and confidence in their future, was when in Baltimore, in 1819, he took up one by one, in calm and deliberate attack, the series of opinions by which Orthodox is distinguished from Liberal Christianity. It was not in the way of learned, critical, scholarly discussion: that he left to men otherwise qualified and gifted. It was simply in the way of eloquent, fervent, elevated appeal against the wrong done to the character of God, the blight put upon the life of man, by a scheme so full (as he regarded it) of unreason, inhumanity, and gloom. The delivery of this discourse was an event, because it publicly enlisted the most eloquent, best known, and most honored minister of Boston on the one side as against the other; because it did more than any other one thing to crystallize the forces and convictions of the liberal party among New England Congregationalists, then only beginning to be known as Unitarians.

To what might be called the speculative side of this movement Channing did not make any very distinct contribution of thought. His sympathies were large and liberal; his opinions in matters of theology were simply the common thought of the more serious, devout, conservative of those who had outgrown the ancient creed. His intellectual method was a firm but gentle dogmatism. Religious truth with him was more a matter of contemplation than of study or clear definition. Natural or critical science he knew very little about. He was content with great vagueness of view, provided the religious want of his mind was fairly met. Thus he hovered always on the edge of an Arianism in which a soberer thinker would hardly find rest or satisfaction; and was content to say that we know too little about the ultimate nature of matter to criticise the story of the Ascension. His strong points were not these; but those wide and generous views of the Fatherhood of God, the Brotherhood of Man, the Dignity of Human Nature, the Free Communion of the ideal Church, which made the theme of discourse in several volumes of eloquent and noble sermons, and constitute still the best body of practical divinity that the Unitarian movement in this country has produced.

It was in the midst of these labors, and in the second period (as I have called it) of his public life, that he sounded the first distinct note of that practical Christian philanthropy with which his name has been most widely and honorably connected, in a sermon on that most sacred and beneficent mission among the poor begun by his near friend, Joseph Tuckerman. This has been the most characteristic, the best organized, and by far the most successful co-operative work that the Unitarian body has ever attempted by way of Church action. Perhaps Channing's word did as much as any man's to dignify and endear it in the heart of its munificent supporters to this day, a little less than fifty years.

From this the step was easy to those questions of Temperance and Education which now began to show themselves in new shapes; and from these again to those which lay upon the border line of morals and politics,— namely, War and Slavery. The spirit and the main line of argument with which he would approach such topics as these may easily enough be taken for granted, as soon as we know his general cast of thought. Happily for him, the public temper had not become so roused and jealous regarding any of them as it has been since; and though there was some regret, some remonstrance, some resentment perhaps, yet there was not the angry hostility which even the gentlest word on some of these matters would have been sure to provoke a few years later.

But the subject which I have named last deserves more special mention : partly because since Channing's day Slavery has gone through its terrible crisis to its stormy end; and partly because without it, and the part he bore in it, though we might have known the beauty, fervor, and elevation of his character, yet we should not have known its moral manliness, determination, and strength.

It was slowly, and in a sense reluctantly, that
one of his temper was drawn to take part in a discussion of such wide public issues, and to identify
himself — he, in his gentle seclusion, and well past
the prime of his years — with a party whose methods
he strongly dissented from, whose uncompromising
creed he never adopted, and whose appeal to passion
he deeply dreaded and condemned. For some six or
eight years the antislavery movement had been under
way. Its principle of abstract justice, its resolution,
its intrepid courage he admired, and he had submitted
to some mild censure because he did not openly take
its ground.

The event that brought him to the front, and made
him afterwards the most intellectually eminent leader
of that movement, was the death of Lovejoy, shot in
defending his press at Alton, Illinois, in 1837. A
citizens' meeting was called at Faneuil Hall, to speak
the word and rally the courage of men alarmed at the
character of the struggle, and especially at what so
threatened the freedom of public debate. Public
opinion set very strongly then, and was as strong in
Boston as anywhere, against any discussion of the
right and wrong of slavery. The Attorney-General
of Massachusetts volunteered on the platform to attack the movement in very bitter and offensive terms.
It was at this speech that Wendell Phillips, then with
all his brilliant oratorical gifts a young man comparatively unknown, sprang to the floor, where his speech
gleamed like flashes of lightning across the stormy
debate, and at one bound took his place at the very
head of platform orators, which he has held, unchal-

lenged, ever since. To those who were there (as I have heard it described), it was an apparition more splendid than any transformation scene upon the stage. On the same occasion Dr. Channing, with a physical hardihood he had perhaps never shown before, stood side by side upon the platform with Garrison and other antislavery leaders whose method he had condemned, but in whom he now saw the champions of that freedom of speech which must be upheld, he thought, by all good men.

This act identified him at once with the principles of that party, though not with its method or doctrine. It enlisted a great amount of moral sympathy and support to the movement; and it committed him to the discussion, which he followed up in six or eight of the most labored and vigorous efforts of his life. A brief treatise on Slavery, dealing with it purely on grounds of moral argument; a public letter of sympathy to Mr. Birney, then the standard-bearer of the Abolition party in politics; a letter to Mr. Clay on the annexation of Texas, which the writer thought cause enough to justify disunion; a letter on Mr. Clay's political position; a tract on Emancipation; and an argument on the duty of the Free States, — this was the series of writings which made Channing, in his later years, the best known exponent of the growing hostility to slavery. Something of popularity and something of comfort he doubtless forfeited; but to one of his temper that was a very small thing, and, sheltered as he was in a thousand ways, could not have touched him very nearly. The obloquy and the personal danger were for hardier fighters in the field. His glory was, that he was content to share their reproach, and that with steady fidelity he served an unpopular cause which he thought right. At least, if his sensitive nature felt keenly (as it did sometimes) the coldness and the unpardoning prejudice of former friends, the world at large was not allowed to know that he suffered; and this, too, was more than made up by the honor widely paid to his integrity and courage.

Years came upon him while his thought was still fresh and clear, and his temper unclouded by infirmity or pain. Some one asked him what he thought the pleasantest time of life. " About sixty-two," he answered, cheerily. A few weeks later, October 2, 1842, it was his great privilege to pass away, almost painlessly, from an attack of autumn fever, — the sunset of his life as calm and radiant as its sunshine had always been. His last public act was an address in memory of West India Emancipation, at Lenox, two months before his death. Its closing sentences are as fine an example as any, both of his style of religious eloquence, and of that fervent hopefulness of spirit which never left him: —

" I began this subject in hope, and in hope I end. I have turned aside to speak of the great stain on our country, which makes us the by-word and scorn of the nations ; but I do not despair. Mighty powers are at work in the world. Who can stay them? God's word has gone forth, and it cannot return to him void. A new comprehension of the Christian spirit, a new reverence for humanity, a new feeling of brotherhood and all men's relation to the common Father, — this is among the signs of our times.

We see it : do we not feel it ? Before this, all oppressions are to fall. Society, silently pervaded by this, is to change its aspect of universal warfare for peace. The power of selfishness, all-grasping and seemingly invincible, is to yield to this divine energy. The song of angels, ' On earth peace,' will not always sound as fiction.

"O come thou kingdom of heaven, for which we daily pray ! Come, friend and saviour of the race, who didst shed thy blood on the cross, to reconcile man to man and earth to heaven ! Come, ye predicted ages of righteousness and love, for which the faithful have so long yearned ! Come, Father almighty, and crown with thine omnipotence the humble strivings of thy children to subvert oppression and wrong, to spread light and freedom, peace and joy, the truth and spirit of thy Son, through the whole earth !"

IV.

FIFTEEN YEARS OF CONTROVERSY.

WHAT we may call the second period in the
history of Unitarianism in this country extends from the year 1836, which showed the first open
breach between the historical and the spiritual interpretation of Christianity, to 1860, when all minor
controversies were suspended in the hush of waiting
for the more terrible conflict just then about to
begin.

But a line may be drawn to define rather more
precisely the period of interior conflict, which made
these years so critical in the history of the Unitarian
movement. It happened that two controversies, which
made a great noise at the time, coincided almost exactly with the date of Channing's death, — the "Pierpont controversy" (which in form was at first simply
a personal dispute respecting the legal rights of a minister, under the old law of settlement, as against his
parish), on the ground of Temperance and moral reform ; and the "Parker controversy," on the ground
of Rationalism and theological reform. It happened,
again, that in 1857 some sort of reconciliation of the
two hostile methods in theology was attempted in the
way of scientific criticism, in the "Christian Examiner," then the leading journal of liberal thought,

under the editorial direction of Dr. Hedge. So that, as regards the interior history of Unitarianism here, the controversial period may be taken as lasting about fifteen years.

This, however, is far from being the only, or even the chief, significance of that term, as applied to the period in view. What has been called "the great controversy of States and people," the half-century debate on the political rights and moral wrongs of slavery in America, was just now at its height. The annexation of Texas in 1845, the Mexican war which quickly followed, the compromise of 1850, including the fugitive slave law, the repeal of the Missouri compromise in 1854, the Kansas struggle in 1856, were the prelude to the appalling conflict into which all passions and interests were drawn for the years 1860 to 1865. From a moral, slavery already became a national question. It had gone frankly upon the field of politics early in the period we are considering, and so belonged no more in particular to the development of opinion in this or any other religious body. It is quite accurate enough for our purpose, then, to mark off these fifteen years from 1842 to 1857, as in a special sense the years of controversy within the Unitarian body.

But I will go back for a moment, first, to the date I began with,—about 1836, the time immediately before the outbreak of these questions. The theological task of old Unitarianism was done, and it had got, or seemed to have got, a good working faith. The shocking and appalling excrescences of the old theology it had removed once for all, for us, by a criticism not very searching or profound, perhaps, but at least quite sufficient for its task. Things painful and incredible in the Biblical record it had either explained away in good faith, or unsuspectingly ignored. The critical movement had gone just so far, that our theory of Christianity was thus absolutely divested of everything that shocked the conscience or common-sense; while its hold on habitual reverence, and faith in its special sanction and authority were absolutely unimpaired. The immense advantage to peace of mind and strength of character was retained, which consists in clinging to a visible symbol honestly believed to be divine, while any suspicion of weakness in the intellectual foundation was left for future finding out. For the present, there was the tranquil and grateful sense of intellectual rest.

But the moment of intellectual rest is only a moment; then comes the next inevitable step of intellectual advance. I say, inevitable. For what we call *rest*, in living things, is like the dead-point of an engine, — a moment of balance, broken in a moment by the same play of the machine that brought it on. What we call *motion* is the effort which the living creature makes to adjust itself to changes that come about not by its choice or will, — changes within, from the law of its structure; changes without, which it must meet or else perish. It is so with the simplest vital motions; it is so, too, with those movements of thought which affect the deepest springs of character, belief, or hope, and which we call religious. But here the effort to meet the inevitable change is more than a vital instinct: it is often a struggle to keep one's hold on a faith which he feels slipping from his grasp; which, if he let it go, takes with it very largely the best comfort and blessing of his life.

I shall not pretend to do again what has been done several times so well already, — to trace the series of those inevitable steps. But it may be observed here, that the conservative instinct, which knows and dreads the impending change, is in its own way far more clearly prophetic than that brave spirit, loyal to ideas, which goes blindfold, as it were, in the paths of Providence. The forebodings of both coward and patriot were far outdone by the terrors of the Wilderness, and the horrors of Andersonville. For those who scouted the forebodings and scoffed the utterers of them, it is the chief honor now to have bravely faced the terror when it came. Happily they could not know that their sanguine hope must be proved at so sore a cost.

So with the warnings of Orthodox foes or timid friends in our theological domain; so with the sanguine hope that hailed the first ray of broadening light. We were warned that we stood on the perilous edge; that a single step would take us beyond the recognized boundaries of Christian faith. There were two directions in which that step might be taken; and each, to those who took them, seemed vital and necessary, not simply innocent and safe. The transcendental free-thinker was sure that his new philosophy gave him a better ground of Christian faith than any external evidences; the liberal critic would only relieve Christianity of a burden and an encumbrance that still hindered its free course to victory. Both were conscious alike of the vast interval which separated their motive from that of the Deistical movement, of evil memory to them both. So both disdained the warning; both overstepped the limit which each had acknowledged as the boundary of Christianity and unbelief; and, in a certain way, both have entered on a larger heritage.

The first shock to the received liberal theology of the day, I should be inclined to say, was Professor Noyes's argument on the Messianic interpretation of the prophecies, in 1834; and the next, Professor Norton's rejection, on grounds part speculative and part critical, of the first two chapters of Matthew, in 1840. That is, these decisive first steps were taken by deliberate, conscientious, conservative scholars, — the best and soberest scholars we had to show. All the rest, we may say, followed as matter of course. But I well remember the mental distress felt by my beloved and honored relative, Henry Ware, Jr., at Mr. Emerson's superb address before the Divinity School in 1838, and the pain with which he listened to his daughter's reading of that tender, reverent, thoughtful exposition of Dr. Furness touching the apparition of angels at the open sepulchre. These are waymarks and memories of the time when a new departure was set unmistakably before the faithful and grieved eyes of the good men who still abode in the former ways. As to the course that has been taken since, I am sure that I speak in the name of a good many who have followed it as far as anybody, when I say that it has been with no iconoclastic zeal and with no sense of triumph over a decaying superstition, but with deep reluctance and regret, and a great sense of personal loss, that they have felt the ancient supports give way which had sustained so much integrity of life and vital piety, and have found themselves, as it were, in the case of pioneers, with a weary track to cross before they could look again for so well-sheltered and fair a home.

It is necessary now to go back for a moment and speak very briefly of those two intellectual movements just alluded to, which brought us, by their irresistible drift, into that period of controversy.

The first was what is called New England Transcendentalism. Its history has been written in a very graceful way by Mr. Frothingham, with warm appreciation of the chief actors in it, and I shall make no attempt to repeat it here.[1]   A mere outline of facts

---

[1] The circumstances which led to the formation of what came afterwards to be known as the Transcendental Club were these. After the public exercises of the Harvard University Centennial, Sept. 8, 1836, it chanced that R. W. Emerson, George Ripley, F. H. Hedge, and George Putnam met in conversation on the unsatisfactory condition of Unitarian theology, and passed the afternoon in conference in a room at "Willard's." The meeting was adjourned to meet at Mr. Ripley's in Boston the following week ; and thence again, in the course of the same month, to Mr. Emerson's in Concord. On this occasion there was a much larger gathering, including A. B. Alcott, C. A. Bartol, G. P. Bradford, O. A. Brownson, W. H. Channing, J. F. Clarke, J. S. Dwight, Convers Francis, Caleb Stetson, Margaret Fuller, and Miss E. P. Peabody. The club thus formed, without rules or organization (sometimes called among its members the "Hedge Club"), continued to meet at irregular intervals, according to personal convenience, — Mr. Hedge living at that time in Bangor, Maine, — for about ten years, or till the abandonment of the Brook Farm experiment, and the removal of Mr.

would tell next to nothing about it to those who did not know it already; and a fair judgment of it would be too long and difficult a task, even if I were otherwise capable of it. The easiest way of describing it is as the sentimental, mystical, and poetic side of the liberal movement. It had its vagaries, its eccentricities, its unintelligible speculation, its fantastic poetry, its wonderful " Orphic Sayings," and its socialistic experiment at Brook Farm; and all these occasioned more or less bewilderment, scandal, or amusement to outsiders. Even the noble and sweet music of Emerson's discourse only made it palatable to the ear, without commending it to the intolerant common-sense of the day; while the great moral sweep and energy of Carlyle, chief prophet of the new era, so full of bracing vigor to the younger generation, hardly began to be recognized under the clumsy humor and unpardonable caprices of his style.

Whatever else may be said of it, this at least may be fairly claimed for Transcendentalism: that it dissolved away a good many hard boundaries of opinion; it melted quite thoroughly the crust that was beginning to form on the somewhat chilly current of liberal theology. Rational criticism is indeed necessary, in order that the current shall move at all; but rational criticism alone is shallow and sterile. If independent thinking is to be united with any fervor and flow of the religious life, it must find religion somewhere as a primary sentiment in human

Ripley to New York. Theodore Parker had joined meanwhile, and Mr. Putnam ceased to attend after the first meeting in Concord. The publication of " The Dial " was begun in 1840.

nature, and not as a mere logical inference from certain facts of history. This is just what New England Transcendentalism did. It was fortunate that it came before the scientific development, and not after it. It is the great felicity of free religious thought in this country, in its later unfolding, that it had its birth in a sentiment so poetic, so generous, so devout, so open to all the humanities as well as the widest sympathies of philosophy and the higher literature, as that.

It is simple and easy justice to say this now, at the end of forty years. But at that time, and for many years later, Transcendentalism was not only a laughing-stock. It was also the great theological bugbear of the serious and devout. As a system of opinion (if such it could be called), it was simply this. The fundamental ideas which make the basis of the religious life, — the idea of God, of duty, and of immortality, — the transcendentalists asserted, are given outright in the nature and constitution of man, and do not have to be learned from any book or confirmed by any miracle. In one way, this followed, easily enough, from what Channing had taught of the dignity and the divine elements of human nature. In another way, it was connected with a certain effervescence of interest and enthusiasm at the new ideas that came floating in, when German poetry and philosophy began to be familiar. It would be no doubt interesting to follow this up on its literary side, since it has deeply colored one large department of our literature, best represented by Emerson and Lowell; but at present we have to do only with its bearing

on theology, and, in fact, only with the negative side
of that.

For it follows, as soon as you state the principle
which lies at the base of the transcendental doctrine,
that you have cut away — like a balloon, as it were
— not only from the ground of narrow common-sense,
but from the moorings of religious tradition. Transcendentalism seemed to affect a certain aristocratic
disdain of common ways of thinking, and to the sober-
minded appeared full of vagary and peril. God, it
said, is not a Being apart from the universe, but
everywhere, as the life of all things, and especially
in your own thought of the Infinite. That sounds
well; but, to the plain understanding of plain people,
"everywhere" is much the same as nowhere, and a
God who is merely infinite is much the same as no
God at all.

So much the worse for the understanding, replied
the transcendentalist: you must learn to discard that,
if you would deal with these high matters, and trust
not reasoning, but only the absolute Reason, "with a
capital R." Reason will teach you that God is not
here or there, but everywhere; there is neither Past
nor Future with him, but only an eternal Now. Not
this or that thing is a miracle, but everything or else
nothing: at any rate (to borrow Parker's illustration),
the real miracle is not turning a few gallons of water
into wine at Cana, but turning hundreds of thousands
of barrels of water into wine every year in France
and Italy and along the Rhine. Duty is taught us by
the voice within: what do we need of the Ten Commandments? We know by our own consciousness

that we are immortal: what need of any proof from the Resurrection? All men are inspired more or less, every man as much as his nature is capable of being: we owe no particular respect to any sacred books, or prophets, or apostles, or to Christ himself, except where our Reason affirms the same truth to us. In short, for all creed or doctrine or inspiration or testimony offered from abroad, Transcendentalism substituted an off-hand dogmatism of its own, whose only evidence was Sentiment, — *I feel that it is true;* or absolute Reason, — *I know that it is true.*

All this was very exhilarating to those young people, especially, who craved religious satisfaction, yet found themselves dissatisfied with the ordinary proofs, which probably they had never investigated or tried to understand. But, as may well be believed, it sounded like blasphemous nonsense to the serious, intelligent, and excellent people who had been trained to a very conscientious acceptance of a revealed religion. As long as it kept in the region of poetry or sentiment or lofty assertion it could be borne with, though it looked a little hazy and rather suspicious. In fact, its serene optimism was already making great havoc of men's plain, old-fashioned theories of right and wrong. But the innocent-sounding, idyllic sentiment became quite another thing when it took shape in one of the most dogmatic of thinkers, sturdiest of combatants, boldest of assailants, most widely informed of students and readers, and in his hands became a sharp weapon of attack.

The war of words which had been long gathering

broke out early in the year 1841, over a thin pamphlet called "The Transient and Permanent in Christianity,"—an ordination sermon by Theodore Parker,
preached in May of that year. There was nothing
in it new to intelligent readers then; nothing that
would not seem harmless enough now, or even commonplace, considering the turn discussions have taken
since: nothing, that is, except the rare rhetorical
beauty, the fervor of sentiment, and the fearless
range of illustration, — those literary qualities in
which Theodore Parker stood out at once far in advance of Channing or any of the writers of his school,
and created, it is not too much to say, a theological
style of his own. That style had great qualities, and
it had great faults. With a singular poetical sweetness, wealth, and fervor, it was vigorous, straightfor-
ward, manly, never a word without definite purpose
and aim; at the same time too self-asserting, too
scornful of antagonists, utterly unmindful of the qual-
ification which sober argument demands, passionate
in conviction, unable to acknowledge truth or honesty
on the other side.

The "permanent" in Christianity was, of course,
its moral doctrine and its religious life; the "transient" was the form, the creed, the fable and myth
wrought about it. The assertions of the discourse
might be borne with, but its illustrations were a deep
offence. That Jesus as Son of God should be likened
to Hercules, and his miracles to those of that errant
spiritualist Apollonius of Tyana, was not easily to be
pardoned by those who considered themselves to hold
a positive system in Christianity. Nothing, in fact,

is so hard to reconcile with Theodore Parker's sagacity or else his good faith as a controversialist, as his surprise at the scandal and dissent which followed. Allowing for a little vacillation and great general ignorance of modern criticism, the average theologians whom he attacked honestly supposed themselves to stand on ground strictly supernatural, and to maintain that ground by fair historical argument. As a rule, they did not attempt to meet him in fair debate, — which, indeed, most of them were quite incapable of doing. His incredible wealth of reading and ready command of the weapons of debate, to say nothing of his hot, aggressive style of attack, would disarm a platoon of average assailants at a breath. In one sense, it was a pity that the controversy as it actually ensued was wordy, stormy, effusive, sentimental, vituperative, angry, — anything but calm and scientific on either side. Men of equal sincerity, equal goodness, equal intelligence, were arrayed on both sides ; and to this day it appears to me that those took the better part who chose neither side, but watched as patiently and modestly as they might to see the scientific bearings of the question, as they should emerge gradually from the noise and smoke of the field.

The waste of hard feeling and the waste of hard words seem a pity ; but that was inevitable when the debate became popular and personal, — and it had to become popular and personal, to prepare that broader way which has been opened since. The most radical questions — not merely about the doctrinal interpretation of the Bible, but about the nature of inspira-

tion, the possibility of miracles, the very foundation
of our belief in God, duty, or immortality — came
directly into the open field.   It was no longer a discussion among metaphysicians, theologians, critics,
and religionists; but men took sides on it as they
do in politics, from temperament or else personal
feeling.

Theodore Parker's name, accordingly, from that of
a retired student, a fervent, very practical,[1] and somewhat sentimental preacher, at once became that of a
party leader.   His personal qualities enlisted the
strongest feelings of attachment and hostility.   His
personal hits were as much enjoyed on one side as
they were resented on the other.   It was a great sol-
ace to him and his friends to corner his opponents in
some false position, where they would seem to deny
on one side the freedom of opinion they had just
been asserting on the other.   It would have been
fatuity in them, on the contrary, — if their own belief or defence of Christianity as they held it meant
anything at all, — to take a different stand from what
they did.   It would have been far more to their discredit if, at his one challenge, they had suddenly aban-
doned their old position, and, at a leap, passed from
an honest though narrow supernaturalism into the
thin air of Free Religion.   It has never been quite
clear to me whether he really felt the surprise he
showed that they did not so stultify themselves, or
whether he merely wished to put them into an un-
comfortable place by pushing home their seeming

---

[1] One of his sermons while at Spring Street was on the peculiar
duties, trials, and temptations of Milk-men.

inconsistency, and so compel them to review their ground.

So far as the controversy was personal, its story has been well told already, and need not be repeated. The correspondence that grew out of it on his part is sometimes sharply unjust, sometimes noble, generous, and very touching. Whatever his faults as a controversialist, — with all that exasperating sarcasm of lip and style, of which he professed himself quite innocently unconscious, — he was not only one of the most genuine, but one of the most affectionate, generous, and warm-hearted of men. The controversy, as he said, and probably felt, was none of his making or choice. So far as it was merely theological, it has greatly lost its interest now that Transcendentalism is out of date, and all discussion of that matter goes upon quite a different set of principles, and a scientific method which was as foreign to the one side as to the other. At bottom, his system was dogmatism resting on sentiment; that of his opponents was dogmatism (in a very mild form) resting on revelation. Both have been taken up and absorbed in a far wider intellectual method, or else are submitted to quite other tests of scientific study. The great heretic and iconoclast of thirty years ago has left a name held almost equally in honor by those on both sides of the old line.

For he was something more than an assailant and a critic. He was a man of great warmth of affection; of rare, fervent, and genuine religious feeling; of broad popular sympathies; capable of great and passionate force of moral conviction. When some of his friends, resenting the petty hindrances and jealousies that blocked his speech, passed the curt and emphatic resolve, "That Theodore Parker shall have a chance to be heard in Boston," and so opened for him the way to a noble metropolitan audience, and a hearing through the press such as was given to no other man of his time, he went on in that open way, not to a futile and petty bickering of theological dispute, but to a work of vast moral sweep and power, which made his the most potent and commanding voice in that larger, more momentous, and fateful controversy in which the main strength of his life was spent.

But, to approach that controversy fairly, it is well to go back to its antecedents in a calmer time. The great debate of human rights and political justice, from forty to twenty years ago, narrowed more and more towards a life-and-death struggle with American slavery. It is impossible for a later generation to understand the sincere repugnance and horror with which that conflict was seen to be approaching; or how what looks now like cowardly compromise and subterfuge seemed to many then their patriotic duty; or how the very things that checked and delayed the antislavery movement were what made the bloody success of emancipation possible.

Historically speaking, it is not nearly so important that all good men should take the view which abstractly seems truest and best, as it is that they should be honest in maintaining their own view, which with the majority of them is very likely, regarded abstractly, neither truest nor best. A party consisting

of all good men on one side, as against a party consisting of all bad men on the other, would be not
only a monstrosity, but a great calamity to mankind.
That slow process of thirty years, by which a majority of American minds were educated to see the
wrong and danger of slavery, was none too slow, if
we think of the conflicting interests and the conflicting forces that were to be plunged into the fight. Of
course, the excited combatants do not see it so. Hot
partisans on either side clamor to exterminate the
leaders of the other. The decision can be had only
when the passions on both sides have been worked
up to striking heat: then the task is taken from the
hands of Reason, and given over to the ordeal of
Battle.

While the debate is going on, two kinds of honest
minds are equally necessary, — the bold, valiant, uncompromising, single-hearted in devotion to an idea,
who are the honest Reformers; the calm, reasonable,
just, able to trim the balance, to watch the chances,
and prevent the infinite hazard and mischief of a
reckless move, who are the honest Conservatives.

But, besides these two, there is a third class, nobler
and more necessary than either. It consists of men
of large intellect and powerful understanding; of
knowledge broad and various; richly equipped by
education and training; allied by natural gifts and
culture to the classes that incline most strongly to
conservatism; yet compelled by clear intellectual
conviction — as Milton was — to cast in their lot,
when the critical moment comes, with the leaders of
a radical reform. Such men distinctly set aside their

own calmer and perhaps better judgment of the circumstances, in view of the one great overwhelming necessity that is upon them to act. Voluntarily they narrow the breadth of their understanding, as their sacrifice to the one idea that just then must be upheld at all hazards. If in the debate which follows they appear narrow-minded, unjust to opponents, violent, positive, self-asserting, it is against the generosity of their nature and the instincts of their breeding. It is, in short, their way of sacrifice to the higher law of necessity and the duty of the hour.

Of such men, the nobler sort of leaders in the great battle of right and wrong, the most eminent among us were Charles Sumner and Theodore Parker. Of all our highly cultivated men of letters, they, I think, were the only ones who gave themselves heart and soul to the antislavery movement as the one chief thing; of all the antislavery leaders, they were the only ones who kept up their broad scholarship, and their interest in all topics, intellectual and moral, that make for the welfare of mankind. And in the period to which I especially refer, — coming down, that is, to some three years before the war,—the place of Theodore Parker was one that belonged to him alone.

It is not, however, my intention to give here a sketch of his character, or of the very able, intense, and incessant labors which broke down his sturdy physical strength, and laid him in the grave before the age of fifty. His is quite too large and remarkable a personality to be discussed in this incidental way. My business now is with the controversy in its general drift, — not as it belongs to the history of the nation, but as it connected itself with the tone of feeling and affected the fortunes of Unitarianism.

We note that, here as elsewhere, there were two exactly opposite tendencies brought into close contact. On the one hand, the Unitarian body, by position and history, was mainly conservative: so far as it included scholars, professional men, merchants, politicians, almost necessarily so. Its theology might be more free in some regards, but in average temper it fully shared the conservatism of all religious bodies then. It is but timidly and awkwardly, in this country at least, that a church deals with matters belonging to the State or to society at large. And what was a violent reproach then, in the mouth of those who thought everything must give way before this one great question of humanity, and cried out loudly against the Church as the "refuge of oppression" because it did not lift up its voice as a trumpet against negro slavery, is easily seen, in all ordinary affairs of State, to be the only right, safe, and possible thing.

A very great stress of personal conviction alone can justify, in any man, the breaking of that safe rule which declares that "within his beat" he may be useful and perhaps strong; outside of it, he may easily do mischief, and will at any rate be weak. All this is to say, in so many words, that the conservative attitude of many churches, during most of the anti-slavery debate, even if carried to a cowardly extreme, was probably conscientious in the main, and was at

any rate inevitable. Right or wrong, that conservative attitude in State affairs was held by most Unitarian churches of any large name or influence; and it
made the hard rock against which more than one
generous heart, bolder if not truer than the rest, broke
itself in vain.

This fact stirred more deep feeling at the time, and
is to this day more blamed and wondered at, than
anything else in the attitude of Unitarianism. It is,
indeed, common to say that those who were not Abo-
litionists then deeply deplore their mistake now, and
wish they had been. But I do not think that this is
at all the case, — certainly not with those who (like
Dr. Gannett) took that conservative ground from
strong and sincere conviction. Most of them, it is
true, were strongly committed to the national cause
in the war for the Union, and heartily sustained the
policy which at last gave the death-blow to slavery.
But those same men would have held it a horrible
crime to declare war for the abolition of slavery, or
to do anything, knowingly, to hasten such a war.

War is a political, not a moral act; and the motive
for it, they held, should be political, not moral. Abstract justice, social right, belong to that kingdom
which is "not of this world," for which it is not
lawful to fight with the weapons of brute force. The
unlawfulness of war, the gospel of peace, had been
taken very much to heart by the earlier generation of
liberal Christian thinkers. The only case that would
justify war, in their view, — the only case that would
seriously perplex the conscience of the more scrupulous, — was the case which really did happen, when

war was manifestly the one thing that could save the nation's life, and when the nation itself was on the right side in a fundamental question of humanity and justice.

I do not think, therefore, that the more conservative of those days have ever repented their alarm and protest at a course of action which seemed to them sure to bring on a civil war, — as, in fact, it did. But, on the other hand, liberalism in theology was the natural ally of liberty and justice in national affairs. The authority of the Creed once shaken, Humanity becomes the strongest sanction of belief and conduct. Political justice becomes necessarily a part of the free-thinker's religion, so long as he has any. It was so with the liberal movement here. Political justice had made part of its history in the Old World, and had been eloquently expounded by a whole generation of the liberal preachers, Channing at their head.

Thus a "gospel of humanity" — sanguine, hopeful, devout — had made a part of the liberal tradition. In seeking to state it to ourselves, we think first of Channing, — his fervent assertion of the dignity of human nature, the glow of his steady hope in the spiritual and social destinies of mankind. And I think we have seen in the older men of that school — older than ourselves, but his disciples — a certain glow of humanity which stayed with them through life, which the chill of old age or long waiting had little effect to quench, as those who have lived in the tropic zone keep something of its warmth through the long frosts of a northern winter. In a certain childlike way it was strikingly so with my father, who quite honestly felt that the years from seventy to eighty were his happiest years. In a still more marked way it was so with that brave saint of all the humanities, Samuel Joseph May, of whom they that loved him may say that only to know him was a sort of sunshine in one nook, at least, of the most unfriended life.

It is worth while to recall the halo which invested that phase of our mental life, that glow as of dawn which hung round the horizon, so as to relieve against it certain phases in which life has shown itself since. Daylight is better than dawn for most uses, particularly for seeing our way among things that bewilder and delude; but it can never have "the glory of the rising." That fair dawn was the opening of a stormy day. The abstract principle, the fervid sentiment that made it, had to be tried as by fire. A season of passionate conflict ensued before the season of calmer reason, of reconciling science. That time of controversy it has not been my purpose to narrate in its events; only to indicate the spirit out of which it grew, and the part had in it by those intellectual leaders who have left their mark deepest upon that time.

Among those leaders, however, I wish to recall very briefly the memory of two marked men with whom I was thrown into rather close relation quite early in the period I have retraced; whose paths crossed not far from then; who both took a very conspicuous part in the movement we are looking back on; who did their task with equal honesty and daring, with

temper not very unlike, but with a difference in aim
and result which went on widening to the end. Of
one of them I have spoken at some little length
already, and shall have occasion to speak again.

Theodore Parker's intellectual self-assertion — remarkable in one who knew so well the history of
human opinion — might be plausibly associated with
the much solitary reading of his youth, without the
chance of conflict and comparison which college
gives; just as his great wealth of sympathy made one
who was honored by it feel as if drawing on the un-
claimed stores of it hoarded in the heart of a childless man, — which, to his frankly expressed grief, he
was. Never did a strong nature show a deeper craving for personal affection, and the exercise of that
power to guide which flows with it. Never did a
strong and passionate conviction hold itself more
patiently in abeyance in intercourse with a younger
mind, lest it should even hint an opinion that might
check its own free working. If not of the first order
of speculative ability, few could be better stored
than he with the positive results of speculation; yet
of all men in that field I should think that none could
have held his religious opinions more absolutely as
postulates admitting no debate, and wholly outside
of any process of argument which may have led to
them.

These opinions were implied throughout in the
polemics that so swept him aside from the studious, constructive work he had marked out, — for
the ambition of his life was to be an historian of
religious opinion, — and with great human passion

made him so genuine an iconoclast. Yet there was noticeable, in his later life, a desire to understand, and a leaning of sympathy towards, some materialistic forms of thought widely alien from his own: either because other men's bigotry offended him, or that he would free his soul from the last trace of theological prejudice.

It was a temporary work, just then greatly needed, that his generous and large nature took upon itself; and his name, it may be, is best recalled as that of a great personal force in the best life of our time rather than as the intellectual leader and guide he doubtless hoped to be. His temperament did not admit of justice towards those who honestly differed, as good men did, in theological opinion or public policy. With the most generous human feeling, he could not pardon the seeming want of it in other men; yet he could bear patiently the argument or the rebuke that tried to convince him he was in the wrong. For high courage I hardly know where we should find his match among men of intellect. It was a moment in history to see him face, with taunt and defiance, an angry crowd in Faneuil Hall, where the Boston regiment mustered on its way to the war in Mexico. And when he went to rest, in 1860, just before the great political triumph of the cause he died for, we missed the clearest and boldest voice of all that read to unwilling ears the stern lesson of the time.

The hard, restless, implacably honest, and domineering temper of Orestes Brownson had just been greatly softened, at the time I first knew him, by a sudden flow of religious feeling in channels which he had thought dried up. A mere accident, as it were, had turned him from a very positive disciple of the French Eclectics to an equally positive and unsparing critic of them in the name of a new teacher (Pierre Leroux), whose phrases he presently took for the key to a new rendering of the Christian revelation,— a reading of it which, with a certain pious and grateful fervor, he detailed in a letter to Dr. Channing on " The Mediatorial Life of Jesus." Beginning his expositions with a sweetness and pathos very marked in so rugged a champion, it was then he uttered the finest sentence of all he ever wrote, in which he spoke of " that glorious inconsistency which does honor to human nature, and makes men so much better than their creeds."

But it was not long before " the old man " in him had its way in vigorous attacks on England and Protestantism. With a curiously slender stock of erudition, he showed an equally extraordinary arrogance and fertility in abstract argument. For example, having toiled with much ado (as he told me) through some fourteen pages of Kant's " Introduction," — having got the idea of it to his own satisfaction, — he proceeded to write more than fifty pages of what, I am told by those more competent to judge than I, is really instructive exposition.

On the 20th of October, 1844, as he told me, he " became a Christian," — that is, a Catholic convert by profession, with all which that name might imply; so that, when I asked him, " But suppose the process that made you a Catholic had been stopped short at a certain point: suppose, for instance, that you had died on the 19th of October?"—"*I should have gone to hell*," he replied, instantly and grimly,—a reply which left neither room for argument, nor, to tell the truth, for interest in any further argument he might have to offer, as soon as one distinctly saw just what the brief was which he had taken in his new appearance before the Court.

Absolute honesty of conviction, a complete cutting adrift from whatever may have been his religious moorings in early life, the weariness of a long war with ideas and customs embedded in modern society, and a religious need craving and imperious as in any zealot of any period, with almost as passionate contempt for the opinions of more knowing but weaker men,—these make it not very strange that a man so strong and arrogant should tire of incessant self-conflict, and choose to enlist his splendid fighting qualities under a flag which at least made him constructively sure of something. But the lesson of his life for us was all told above thirty years ago; and the strong, stormful, rude, yet tender-hearted man passes away, leaving hardly a ripple in our memory to remind us what his influence had been.

I recall these names not idly, but to reinforce the single thought with which I close. None of the topics and none of the questions I have been dealing with are topics or questions of speculative interest merely. It is HUMAN interests, the character, life, work, destinies of men, that come in play, and are touched by them. And perhaps we see this plainest when we remember that there are men who by genius and endowment are leaders of other men, to whom these spiritual things are of incomparably more moment than all personal and terrestrial things; men who willingly — nay, inevitably — renounce and cut adrift from everything else, that so they may save their souls. Also, that whatever is honorable and of good report in the world, and whatever makes the world's life worth living, depends on its having and cherishing that order of men, to whom Circumstance is as nothing, and Thought is all.

V

THEODORE PARKER.

THE names of Channing and Parker stand for very different if not hostile types of religious feeling and belief. But they are constantly mentioned together as representative names. Right or wrong, Unitarianism is everywhere held responsible for them both. One as distinctly recalls the later as the other does the earlier phase of the movement we are attempting to trace. I have hinted already at the attitude of the theologian. I should like, if I may, to bring you into a little nearer acquaintance with the man.

Theodore Parker's biography gives us glimpses of a childhood and youth not greatly different from that of many an energetic and studious country boy in New England. Being the youngest of eleven children, and five years younger than the tenth, it is likely that he had more than his share of his parents' companionship and care. How tenderly and piously his conscience was instructed by his mother, he has narrated himself in the story of the "little spotted tortoise;" and he told me once how his father, when he was eight years old, made him give his childish analysis of Plutarch's Cicero, before allowing him to read another of the Lives. In the charming story of his early years, Mr. Weiss speaks of "the bloom in the down of his young cheeks competing with the fruit as he jogged down the road" to carry his father's peaches to market; and we read how the sturdy youth, trained to all busy and helpful ways, when he left home to teach school or make a visit, would hire a man "to take his place and work on the farm," till he was twenty-one.

As a student here in Cambridge, and in the first years of his ministry, he was not understood to differ in opinion much, if at all, from those about him; though I have heard him say that even as a child the current supernaturalism was never a real belief to him, as it was to most of us. The first public indication of any change was when he had been already five years, or nearly, in the public work of his profession; and, when this proved to be the first step in a radical controversy, he went out for a year's rest — or, rather, for busier study and observation — in Europe. So that there was not haste, but rather great deliberation, in his entering upon the work that made him so speedily and widely known.

From his return in 1844 until the fatal attack which forced him from his post in January, 1859, was a term of almost exactly fifteen years, during which he did his most effective and characteristic work. Fifteen years are a term so short, that there were those old enough to take a share in that work from the first, and to go with him all the way, who yet might feel at the end of it that their own task was not much more than begun. His unusual bodily vigor and capacity of labor might promise at least twice as long a term, and he probably expected to work on till seventy without much abatement. That he broke down as he did at forty-eight, means not merely that he was vulnerable to the disease fatal to so many of his kin. It means also an unsparing, even prodigal, spending of his strength. It means, too, that something of his strength was wasted needlessly. Seeing a sounding-board above the pulpit in a Swiss church during his last journey, he said, sadly, "If I had had that in Music Hall, I should not be here now!" But, to tell the truth, his voice was used un-skilfully; throat and lungs were rasped by the effort to speak too loud. This we may say now in pity and regret, honoring the motive of it all the more. For it was of a piece with the rest. His life was poured into his work wholly and at once. Not only the water was always moving, but the channel was always full. Prudence would say, Economize the power; do not spend the wealth of life so fast; more will be done at last if done less prodigally at first. But a motive higher than prudence — what in certain cases we may call the Divine economy of life contrasted with the human — will decide otherwise. An effort of massed and concentrated strength is more than the same amount husbanded and diffused. There is no common measure between the force of a pressure and the force of a blow. The true value of a life is often in the intensity of the flame that is burning it away.

The first impression received by one who came in contact with Mr. Parker in the prime of his years was of a nature at once sturdy and kindly. His frame was solid, square-set, hardy, and robust. On a long exhausting journey, on foot or otherwise, after the spirit of his companions flagged, and their strength was spent, late into the day or night, he would go on (it was said) just as cheerily, strong in step, high in spirit, with argument, anecdote, and fun to keep up their failing courage by the way. On the farm, in the handling of scythe or plough, there were few day-laborers who could keep up with him. What would be a severe day's task for any ordinary student he would combine with whatever other work he had to do. Thus, when he taught a country school and supped at five, he would study from six till two. On a lecturing tour he must take his satchel full of books, to be devoured at odd times upon the road. As a member of this School, I do not venture to say what his industries were; but I have heard him tell with relish of the great German theologian who lamented to him that he himself was able to give no more than eighteen hours a day to his books!

In finish of scholarship he doubtless lacked the accuracy which a more critical training would have given. But by patient accumulation he had stored up a wealth of knowledge that was always a fresh surprise; so that, to one who went to consult him on almost any topic of remote investigation, it was almost as if he had just booked up expressly on the very matter in hand. His mind was curiously informed in special and out-of-the-way fields of knowledge. Details of natural science, the history of law cases (which he had read in great abundance during a winter's leisure), the dry technicalities of the Civil Code, the gossip and minutiæ of contemporary history, the bleak abstractions of metaphysics, seemed to be about equally familiar. Even when suffering severe pain, and holding his head in both hands (as I have seen him), he would lay hold on some topic of thought or knowledge, with the fulness of learning and allusion, and the formal exactness of method he was so fond of, as if he were stating the outline of a treatise or essay.

Still, it was not that singular wealth of erudition you thought of first. What you found in him was rather a powerful, rich, and greatly-gifted nature, to which the gathering and disbursing of its ample stores was only the generous play of its native strength. Accordingly, the capacious understanding was at least balanced by emotion and active energy. That large nature clung to personal friendships closer than to any abstractions of the brain. In the midst of his various lore, that heart so opened in love to natural things, that he thought even of an insect tenderly, and knew — as was said of him, with perhaps some friendly exaggeration — every bird and wild-flower in New England. Nay, he took the text so literally, as to say that not a sparrow can fall to the ground but for *that sparrow's* good. In riper years, watching and nursing by a sick bed, or plans of active charity among the poor, or guarding with loaded weapons the liberty of a fugitive slave, or breasting the storm and tumult of an unfriendly crowd in tempestuous controversy, made to such a mind as natural a play of its forces, as easy an assertion of itself, as the gathering up of knowledge or the heat of strenuous debate. The personality was more and stronger than the intelligence. The thought was felt as well as spoken. What, historically, was one phase of the controversy that is always going on between obstinate tradition and fresh conviction was, personally, the blending of thought and emotion, a warm human experience shaping itself into words. It is so that a necessity is laid upon every strong and passionate nature to speak what in its day and hour is given it to speak.

Positive and imperious as that nature was, strong and imperative as was the desire to stamp itself upon the general mind, — nay, unable, as he seemed, to understand or allow for the force of motives in other men who disagreed with him in matters of opinion or conduct, — he was in private intercourse altogether courteous, unobtrusive of his own opinion, generous to the view he most gravely opposed. In argument he might seem uncompromising, intolerant, scornful. Impatient of contradiction, confident in assertion, sharp in denouncing the policy or the man at war with his own view of right, the public could not, very likely, suspect this more intimate and human side of him. But to his friends the memory of it is even stronger than of the other side. In conversation or letter he was apt to speak his mind in the same biting and sarcastic way as in public. Anything cowardly or false, or what seemed so, he could not easily pardon, and perhaps was too quick to suspect. But when he knew that another person was making up his mind honestly for himself, — studying any point of controversy, or debating a question of public morals, — it might be observed that he was careful not to contradict, not to urge his own opinion, not even to present it. A sense of intellectual delicacy and honor would seem to hold him from forestalling, by a word or hint, the freest action of another's mind or conscience.

And so his incidental expressions of his own opinion — more particularly his public ones, which were positive and intolerant — were often curiously at variance with the kindness and courtesy he showed in private to the opposite opinions. Freedom of personal criticism he always said that he valued and wished to hear; and with exceeding patience and kindness, even with a humility which might seem strange to those who knew him less, he would receive the very plain and candid expression of it from one who ventured to take him at his word. Friends of his were pained and disturbed, more than once, during the sharp word-battles of his last ten years, at hasty and unjust judgment publicly spoken of persons they held honorable and dear, and frankly told him so. It was so far a satisfaction and relief to them, that he took all such words kindly; that he always expressed gratitude for any criticism or correction; that in some instances he even yielded as to a point of judgment or feeling, whether or not he gave any public expression of it.[1]

[1] Of this generosity in judgment, which has not generally been recognized in him, my own correspondence with him has several marked proofs. Almost the only exception was in a short letter of his in censure of Dr. Gannett, which to my great regret was published in his biography. As to this, Dr. Gannett says, in a note to me, "I do not know to what information Mr. Parker refers; but, I suppose, to a story which he must have believed, and which I re-

But, again, opinion in him was never wide apart from passion. In private communication his language was always kind and generous, often affectionate, even when dealing with opinions and things he did not love. But in the war of words, where sharp strokes are given and taken, there was no one whose judgments were more colored by personal feeling, no one who showed more temper in argument, or more identified the principles with the persons of his antagonists; no one who made bitterer foes or warmer partisans; no one who carried more of intense and breathing life into the whole disputed realm of technical theology or practical morals.

Still, it was with no hurry or impatience that he entered into the conflict which afterwards absorbed him so completely. Rather it was deliberately, even slowly, after long study, with large training and equipment, after considerable experience in life lived quietly, and after that experience was widened by travel and much acquaintance with men. He was then at the age of thirty-four. He had measured his powers and clearly defined his work. Slowly, almost reluctantly, he was drawn on to that post in the front of the battle, which he held in an attitude so determined, energetic, defiant. " He represented and pro-

member seeing in one or two English Unitarian papers (which I confess vexed me), to the effect that I had said something in the pulpit about the Fugitive Slave Law, which I did not say. Then, as now, they who differed were too eager to misrepresent, and too prompt in misunderstanding one another. Contradiction seldom does much good, and time is the best corrective of mistake." The publicity given to Mr. Parker's letter (Weiss's " Life and Correspondence," vol. ii. p. 110) justifies this personal reference.

claimed a revolution, and devoted all his powers of conscience and understanding to organize the great change by means of timely justice, that he might, if possible, prevent Freedom from stepping to her place through blood."

These words of his biographer sufficiently express the position in which Theodore Parker now stood before the world. But the first task of a reformer must always be with men's motives and their faith. It was inevitable that he should begin as a controversialist and a critic of religious opinion. In this he was unsparing, imperative, scornful in speech, as his nature compelled him to be in dealing with what to him was error. But his positiveness of temper and opinion, his hate of insincerity, his animosity towards views that seemed to him degrading and wrong, grew out of a deep, warm, trustful belief. In a letter answering some inquiry I had made of him in behalf of a friend, in reference to a rumor that he failed to find comfort in his own belief, he gives his own position, as it looked to him, in these words : —

" The great point in which I differ from most Christians is this : I believe in the Infinite God, who is perfectly wise, perfectly just, perfectly loving, and perfectly holy. Of course he must have a purpose in creation, a plan in creation, — both perfect and consistent with this infinite wisdom, justice, love, and holiness. This plan must be adapted to secure the ultimate welfare of each creature he has made, and must be perfect in detail as well as in the sum. How, then, can I fail to find comfort in sorrow, — even in the worst of sorrows, *consciousness of sin ?* I cannot. I have unspeakably more delight in religion, more consolation in any private grief, more satisfaction in looking on the present or for the future, than ever before, when I trembled before an imperfect God. I never said, never thought, never felt the sentiment attributed to me. Quite the contrary."

As with his religious, so with his moral convictions. If in his career of public assault on public wrong he was dogmatic, imperative, scornful, — that grew out of a personal feeling deep and sincere. Moral emotion still more than intellectual conviction was at the heart of his argument on such things. The argument was concrete, living, personal. It was the wrong actually endured by the slave, by the victim of drunkenness or profligacy, by the family of the drunkard, by the crowded and vicious hordes of the neglected poor. In later years especially he connected his moral doctrine very much with theories of ethnology, — that is, the facts of human nature seen on the broadest scale; and with statistics, — that is, the facts of human society gathered and arranged so as to let the underlying laws of them, the great and general facts, be seen. But even in stating them in the widest way historically, or in the precisest way scientifically, or in the most positive way dogmatically, he would never forget, as some do, that they are *human* facts. The statement or discussion would presently be relieved by some flash of sympathy or tenderness or indignation; and the philosopher or reasoner, at the heart and heat of his argument, was always lost in the man.

If we now look back upon the period of time when his public labors began, we shall remember that it was a time when the controversies that have vexed us since had only begun to take on the shape and acrimony we of a later day have found in them. Theological debate was lulled after the strifes of fifty years ago. The churches held each its own position pretty distinctly and quietly. The dispute about old doctrines was subsiding. The more radical questions that have stirred us since had not yet come up, except in the minds of a few who were studying and thinking by themselves. There was a truce in the war of sects and creeds.

The question of Slavery had by no means taken the ominous and dread proportions which it assumed before Mr. Parker's death. Antislavery was an effort, a faith, a sentiment, a hope, with a party comparatively few and unregarded. Emancipation was a new thing in the British West Indies, and we were rejoicing in the peaceable fruits of it so far, blind to the practical difficulties still to be met. At home, the Texas question was laid to rest, and only the more sagacious (like President Adams) knew the drift of party policy which soon opened up so rapidly. Henry Clay had predicted that slavery would come to an end before the end of the century; some sanguine persons thought that ten years more — the middle of the century — would see the question brought to its final issue, and universal liberty the law of the land.

The cause of Temperance was just then entering on its most interesting, glowing, hopeful stage, in the "Washingtonian movement." It seemed now as if the decisive experiment had been made; as if the one needed lesson had been learned; as if the light of safety and hope were brought home, once for all, to those sunk lowest in the bondage of corruption; as if the way were now plain to sweep all the forms of at least one dreadful vice from the face of the land. No suspicion as yet of the long vain struggle, the countless difficulties and mistakes, the license laws and penal laws, action and reaction of the popular mind on all that touches a popular sin, tenacity of habit and depravity of will, variety and cunning of the disguises that cloak the infirmity and shame of a moral malady. How much of all this we were waiting to learn from the experience of the years that were to follow!

And, again, it was a pretty common feeling then that the time had gone by for War — at any rate, war on a large scale — among civilized and Christian powers. It was really believed that the progress of Christianity in general, and the Peace movement in particular, had gone so far as that! Among the more scrupulous and humane, the question whether any forcible resistance to anything is ever right, was a question pressing close upon the conscience, — as if that were likely to be the practical problem next brought forward for solution. But the revolutions of 1848, beginning in an outburst of humanitarian sentiment, opened an era strangely different. To say nothing of six great European wars — in Hungary, in the Crimea, in Italy, in Germany, in France, in Turkey — enlisting our sympathies so strongly on one side or the other, the appalling disasters of our own Civil War have opened to us what deeps below deeps be-

neath that placid surface of mild emotion with which
we then entertained the question of resistance or non-
resistance, of peace and war!

Such was the generally buoyant and hopeful tone
in which the moral questions of the day were then
regarded. We may well confess to a little self-com-
placency, a superficial self-confidence, — as if, after
all, the time of martyrdom had been mostly lived
through; as if the great work of Reform could be
carried on with fine sentiments, and delicate hands,
and hearts safe from the great storms of passion and
fear that had beaten in the past! Some of us well
remember how completely that feeling was uppermost
at the time referred to. The pure fervor of those
words in which Channing closed his last public address did but echo the hopeful and sanguine strain;
did but reflect the aspect in which the gravest issues
were regarded, not merely in the buoyancy of youth,
but in the deliberate conviction of ripe years.

But it is not the way of Providence that any question vitally touching the rights and welfare of humanity, or the progress of Divine truth, should be
settled on such cheap and easy terms. If only that
men may know what their principles are, what depths
of character and experience they involve, it is necessary to hold them as possessions attacked and fought
for. To know the preciousness of truth, it must be
slowly and painfully disentangled from a mass of
error. The battle cannot be won for us at second
hand. Each generation has its own warfare to encounter, and its own victories to win. What seemed
to us then a hopeful, busy, and prosperous advance

towards the easy achievement of truth and right;
what seems now to have been a somewhat superficial
and deceitful mood of moral emotion, or even a lull
and suspension of the struggle, — had to be broken
up. A generation must be passed in the phases of a
conflict about truths which the heart holds dearest
and principles which the conscience holds holiest,—a
conflict of which none can yet see the course or end,
— that a grander work may be done, and a nobler
faith may grow from the roots of a deeper life.

It was just this conflict which Theodore Parker
seems to have been expressly commissioned to open.
He was as early as any one to proclaim it. He threw
himself into it with all the wealth of his understanding, and all the energy of his will. He was so
closely identified with it at every stage that we cannot call to mind a single event, or public act, or critical moment in the whole stir and stress of the period,
in which his voice was not one of the most clear and
decisive, and his word — bold, clear, ready, positive —
was not among the first to arrest the public mind.
And yet he so far shared the general state of feeling
then, that he always said the resistance he met in
the outset was a strange thing to him. He apparently expected to find his words accepted and assented
to at once. He was only carrying out the principles
all liberal thinkers had proclaimed. The one further
service he would render must needs be welcome to
all who professed freedom of opinion in religious
things.

In his earliest discourses addressed to the public
we observe these two things: a positive, dogmatic,

almost disdainful way of laying down the main lines of his argument,—and this as clearly and fully in his very first words as ever afterwards; and, with this, a certain confiding, poetic, sentimental way of stating his ground of "absolute religion," as if the world had only to hear and forthwith accept the new gospel in all its simplicity. These two, strongly marked at first, continued together unabated to the end.

Considering how much of a controversialist he was, how familiar with the history and criticism of every form of belief, how generally known as assailing other men's opinions, it is remarkable how self-confident he always was in asserting his own. It is as if he had never known a doubt. It is as if there were no shading-off in his mind between absolute belief and absolute disbelief,—as in the sky of the tropics there is no twilight, but night shuts down dark against the brightness of the day. As I understood him to say, he never knew that period of transition which most inquirers must pass through. The world of mingled truth and error, of right and wrong, lay before his eye with sharp contrasts of white light and black shadow, —like the surface of the moon, where there is no softening atmosphere, but every shade is a blot of absolute dark on a field of pure and shining white. It did not occur to him that where he and other men differed, he might possibly be mistaken; that there might possibly be some truth — of experience, if not of fact or philosophy — in the doctrine he attacked. And so he hated what to him was error. He could not see any good in things evil, or any right in the fabric built on a foundation he failed to recognize.

With most men, the best part of their religion is far from being that which lies in the clear, glaring light of consciousness, or what they could give the best account of to themselves or others. The twilight atmosphere of mystery in which our lives are wrapped — from clear light shading off imperceptibly to obscurity and gloom — is the sphere where most of our pious thoughts and emotions lie. In Theodore Parker it was almost as if this shadowy sphere did not exist. Where he recognized any truth at all, it was positive, clear, dogmatic, — no half-truth of the emotion merely, no mystery haunting the imagination and secretly magnetizing the thought. Where other men spoke of a hope reaching forth to the after life, a reverent looking forward, a trembling trust, he was ardent, confident, positive. With him, he said, immortality was no wish or dream or hope. It was more than belief: it was knowledge. He *knew* he was immortal: he felt it in every fibre of the soul. Anything less than that was unworthy the name of belief at all. Any demand of proof was an impertinence. Any offer of historical evidence was an affront to the living faith.

So with the love of God for his creatures, and the destiny He reserves for them in a future state. It was not a thing to be waited for and trusted in with awe and trembling, with dread and shame lest we might not be worthy to behold the Holiest and live, — lest the glories of the life beyond might be higher than our aspirations or our deserts. He would embrace without a shade of misgiving, for every man, the prospect of a world beyond the grave. He *knew*

God must mean the best for every creature ; that not even guilt can long be a barrier from His love ; that not the wickedest of men should be ever afraid to die.

Again, the presence and action of God in human life, — it is now, here, always, or else never and no-where. There is no middle ground between atheism and the sense of a present Deity. God's miracles, real miracles, are in the movements of the heavens and in the fresh growth of every spring-time. To set apart any class of events and acts, and call them miraculous, or any special evidence of God's power, is as much as to deny that power in other events and things. The revering and tender associations which make so many cling to the miracles of the New Testament and believe in them — illogically, perhaps; at least, rather with heart than head — had no place with him at all.

Thus his theory of Christianity was far from com-plete, and his judgments of other men were far from faultless. Nor was his theory quite consistent with itself. Especially where he stood most widely apart from the general sense of Christendom, and most gloried in the difference, — in his theory of sin in the soul, — it seems impossible to reconcile his eager op-timism with his godly hatred of all forms of evil in the concrete. But to no man is it given to compre-hend all truth, or to fulfil all righteousness. They have little ground to censure his rejection of the "sa-tanic element" from his theology, who have not shared or excelled the ardor of his moral conviction.

Out of a certain defect in his mind which I have

tried to indicate, he would often seem not in the least to understand or do justice to the minds of others. And so there was a vein of misunderstanding and injustice, on both sides, which made bitter and false a large part of his controversy with the popular theology. I do not remember a single statement he ever made of the doctrine of his opponents which they would be willing to accept, while he did make many statements of their doctrine which they considered wilfully offensive misrepresentations and caricatures. His generosity to the personal character of an opponent whom he deemed sincere made the more remarkable the sarcasm and scorn which he visited upon things dear to their heart and cherished in their faith.

In two directions, especially, his service ought to be thankfully acknowledged even by those who think his fundamental opinions dangerous and wrong. It is in evidence that his words were the first to break the spell of superstitious terror in many a mind that waited only for the trumpet-tone of such a voice to chase away the spectres of an evil dream, and turn religion from a slavish fear into the glad liberty of a child of God. And, again, there was a form of scepticism, an undercurrent of hostility to the popular creed, which was running fast to an open and mocking infidelity, taking more and more a sensual and materialistic tone. The arm's-length and puny opposition which such unbelief as this finds in the paid pulpit of an established creed is a very different thing from the clear, bold word of the independent thinker.

By sheer mental force and wealth of knowledge this man headed the column of insurrection against the Church. But, in doing it, he gave a new type and tone to that hostility. Under his lead heresy became more pious, more thoughtful, more humane than the orthodoxy it opposed. Hundreds were saved from a reckless and blank atheism, because they saw his independent vigor of thought and his unsparing attacks on error joined to a positive faith in the Divine providence and law, an absolute loyalty to right, a confidence clear, ardent, and unwavering in the immortal life of every human soul. It was wonderful how wide his words spread and with what eagerness they were received, — the only words, teaching any free form of piety, that went as far as civilized men followed the narrowing track across forest and prairie, or wherever two or three were gathered together to grope their way out of the tangle and obscurity of the theological growths around them.

In the field of moral and political debate there was one service he rendered which no other did, which perhaps no other could, render so well. He carried into that field all the wealth of a mind very richly stored, a great fund of various erudition, a breadth and masculine vigor of understanding, which redeemed the debate from partisan littleness and lifted it upon the plane of the larger ethics. We know how apt such discussions are to degenerate into mere vaporing declamation, into vituperative wrangling, into pitiful sects and schisms. We know how hard it is even for a rich and highly cultivated intellect, that gives itself wholly to them, to avoid the mistake and harm. Mr. Parker did not entirely escape this danger. There was passion and there was injustice in his speech. But that was the honest flaming-out of moral wrath; and it is a glory to a man to be capable of that!

The great gain was, when a man whose profession and bent of thought turned him towards what is high, abstract, infinite, — whose studies made him at home in the wide field of history, — whose professional walk led him into scholarly and refined circles, as well as among the lowly and the poor, — when such a man stood in the front rank as a champion of moral reform. It was no vague and theoretical moralizing he brought to the great debate, no mere polish of accomplished oratory, no mere denunciation of the evil, or eloquent vindication of the right. It was a masculine judgment of men and things, such that in all records of the sort we have never seen the like. Industry like that of a blue-book, gorgeousness of diction like Burke's, moral passion like that which flames in Milton, might be gathered in a single occasional discourse. There was the massing of materials for other men's independent judgment, and the marshalling of them so that their statement should be an argument. That self-ordained tribunal commanded the attention as much of those who hated and opposed as of those who admired and applauded. Before its terrible bar every event, every deed of evil policy and every prominent actor in it, had to be dragged, to abide something like the verdict of posterity, pronounced by that fearless voice from those unsparing lips. Unsparing of honest prejudice, of gentler feeling — unjust, no doubt, often to the motives of men, and too easily believing ill of them[1] — yet it was a tribunal which extorted hearing and commanded respect.

Thus that breadth of vision, that wide sweep of knowledge, prevented the debate being ever narrowed to party bigotries and sectarian aims. To-day, the boldest words as to some affront from slavery upon the public conscience; to-morrow, a plea for the ignorant, the lowly, the degraded in our own city streets: now, vehement exposure and denunciation of some man's act, or verdict on some man's character, unsparing in its bitterness; and again, some tender breathing of filial piety, some act of delicate sympathy and kindness for distress, some word of gentle consolation to those that mourn and labor and are heavy-laden. Large as was the field of action, rich and various as were the gifts he brought to labor in it, we find in his life a symmetry, a singleness of purpose, a persistency of aim, a consistency of motive, such as we rarely find in far lower and narrower ranges of men's lives. Such a life can well afford to acknowledge greater defects of opinion and graver errors of judgment than can be pointed out in him.

I will return for a single word to the religious tone and motive of the life. Mr. Parker's creed has

---

[1] For example, he persisted in believing the strange calumny (which would be insulting to a border ruffian) — impossible in what it charged, and promptly denied — that Dr. Dewey, a man of the tenderest filial piety, had said he would "send his own mother back to slavery" to sustain the law; and could not be induced to admit that Daniel Webster was honest in dreading a war of Disunion, which he was himself soon after incessantly predicting.

been called "a humane and tender optimism, which strove to embrace all the facts with something like Divine impartiality." If this optimism was strongly contrasted by the intolerant tone he often took in public debate, then on the other hand it is borne out with singular harmony and consistency by what we are permitted to read of his private papers. Force of character needs the nurture of solitude. The minutes of those many lonely midnight hours register with curious precision the steps and processes of that nurture. The one characteristic most marked in them, the one feature of character which perhaps most required just this testimony to make it adequately known, is the incessant reverting to the mood of piety. Aspiration after moral purity, after a fearless and true spirit in doing the work of life, is earnest and constant. If it were not for the immense visible result in the work done and the battle waged, the impression would be almost that of a pietist and a devotee.

Yet this, too, is in strict consistency with his general theory of religious things. Supplication for particular blessings and special "providences," as if the Unchangeable were to be moved by human entreaty, he shunned as idolatrous and profane. Even the phrases of his devotion contain the formal denial of that doctrine of prayer which has been held and argued for so earnestly by many of the most pious men. But if prayer signifies the earnest seeking of the Holiest, "if haply we might feel after him and find him ;" if it implies absolute reliance, joyful confidence, the power both to find and to impart conso-

lation in human griefs from that heavenly source, —
then the "gift of prayer" has been bestowed on few
men in larger measure. Many, who were distant and
strangers in his lifetime, sincerely thought him an
enemy of Christian truth. But such may find in this
record now, if not complete harmony of soul, at least
a deeper life-current, which blended the warmest
springs of devotion in the strength that battled as
rudely against men's cherished beliefs as against their
rooted wrongs. Perhaps it is not too much to say
that in piety of just this type we find the living link
which binds what is purest in past forms of religion
with what is best in those that are to be. If an
"age of reason" is to follow the "ages of faith," it
was well that one brave pioneer should share so
largely in the characteristic life of each.

Theodore Parker broke down in the midst of his
unfinished work, and died before the age of fifty. In
his absolute confidence in the Wisdom and Love that
govern all things, he could call to mind barely one
thing—his childless lot—that he would have wished
otherwise. Almost to the last, he was able to speak
with cheerfulness, even pleasantry, of his passing
strength. Of course, it must have been with one deep
pang of keen sorrow and disappointment. He had
identified his life so completely with his work! and
the task was but hardly begun, even then growing
larger and harder upon his hands. It is the fallacy
of a strong heart and living conscience that God
cannot spare his laborers from their task; that the
work is theirs, not His; that they are responsible
for the result as well as for the deed. In those fifteen

years of strife, had the bondage of bigotry and error been much loosened ? — had the chains of the slave grown any lighter ? — had the curse of intemperance and licentiousness, the dishonesties and inhumanities of trade, the grief of hopeless poverty, been lessened in the community he lived in and labored for? Might it not seem, possibly, as if the labor had been in vain ,— at least, as if a few years more ought to be given, to save it from being lost ?

Questions like these must come — we cannot tell how often or how keenly — when the over-wearied laborer rests at night, and contrasts the scanty harvests of the afternoon with the glow and confident promise of the morning. But a man can live only once. If he has given his own measure of strength, if he has brought his own best gift, it is all that can be asked of him, or by him. Force, say the scientists, is never lost, but only takes new forms. Certainly this is true, if anywhere, then of moral force. He has cast in his own life as one of those innumerable forces by which the life of Humanity is made complete. One is taken, and many another left.

VI.

A SCIENTIFIC THEOLOGY.

THE Secession of 1860, and the Civil War which presently followed, introduced a period in several ways favorable to the liberal movement in theology. It was, in fact, as much a breaking up of old lines of sect, and a liberalizing of the public mind on religious questions, as it was the introduction of a new era in politics. There was a great shaking together of all sorts of opinions in camp-life. In the readjusting of parties, sects as well as sections came to have quite a new understanding of one another. In the heat of the new enthusiasm, old prejudices were fast melted away. Persons before obnoxious for their radicalism now found themselves quite in the current of popular thought. It was no accident that the one great national work of organized charity — the Sanitary Commission — was due to the genius of the best recognized leader of the liberal forces; or that the same week which saw the surrender of Richmond saw also the carrying out of his scheme of a National Conference designed to give new coherence and executive vigor to the loose and scattered ranks of Unitarianism.

There is, accordingly, a very special sense in which the period that has followed, with the wider scale and greater variety of denominational activity, is best represented by the name of Dr. Bellows. His death is quite too recent to let us measure the amount of loss the Unitarian body has suffered by it. But it may be said here, that he saw with singular distinctness both the opportunity offered and the conditions under which it had to be met. His view took in the field, as perhaps no one before him had conceived it, at once so widely and so vividly; and he recognized with great decision, even if he did not formulate, the terms of that larger alliance by which the tasks of liberal theology must henceforth be carried on. His was, besides, one of the few names of great weight that served as living links between the later and the earlier generation. The Unitarian body was greatly fortunate, that, while there were still others to bring it wealth of thought and sufficiency of scholarship, there was this one leader, trusted and beloved, to help it towards a generous breadth of fellowship, and something like energy of concerted action.

But perhaps the period before us is still better characterized by a much younger class of men, who, with less of critical study or defined opinion than their predecessors, have a readiness in action, a vigor of self-assertion, a directness of method, and a range of popular sympathy that set them quite apart from the older school, and give them a new and different hold upon the future. We have especially to recognize a group that are working with great spirit and independence at a distance from what was before the only centre of our action; and another group who have come into the Unitarian body from outside, seeking more liberty of thought, and bringing with them the tradition and the habit of greater religious zeal. The position of the one and the new associations of the other are both favorable to freedom of opinion. Neither of them feels the strong conservative bond of the Congregationalist tradition, or is held so firmly by reverent and loyal memory of honored names.

In short, Unitarianism, so far as it is destined to survive at all, must understand that it has outgrown its old theological limits; and, as it was once the liberal side of the old Congregational body, so now it must know itself as the Christian side of the broader scientific movement of our time. As a part of this broader movement, it may still retain its intellectual dignity and its interest for thinking men, whatever its denominational strength or weakness. Apart from that, it has but a feeble life of its own, and will be soon scattered to pieces, or else merged in the superior energy and the increasing liberality of the larger bodies around it.

That result is freely predicted for it by eager sectarians who oppose it, and by radical thinkers who secede from it. If such a result is to be averted, it must be by maintaining a positive religious life of its own, with its foundation of deep conviction both intellectual and moral; and at the same time by guarding that absolute liberty of opinion, that freedom from theological prejudice and restraint, which will entitle it to move in equal alliance with the science and literature of the time.

Now how far liberty of opinion is consistent with

religious sympathy and harmony of action, is a matter for the present of very doubtful experiment. Most persons, when they speak of liberty of opinion, silently take for granted the limits they themselves respect. Thus the "right of private judgment," with the Reformers of the sixteenth century, included also the "sufficiency of the Scriptures." The freedom claimed by the early Unitarians assumed the whole apparatus of miracle and special revelation. The Reformers did not feel any inconsistency in demanding that freedom of conscience should be within the limits of an evangelical creed ; or the Unitarians, in assuming that it must accept the absolute authority of Christ. Probably we should demur, most of us, at a religious fellowship which should include outright denial of God or immortality, or outright profession of communism or free love, however honest it might be. And when we speak of liberty of opinion, or breadth of religious communion, it seems quite necessary, at starting, to find out how much we really mean by those terms.

It appears to me that the only answer we can give that question, is one which absolutely disclaims the drawing of all lines of religious fellowship at men's speculative opinions about anything. All honest opinions are matter of fair discussion, as between individual minds. I think they should make the lines of division among men only just so far as they correspond with the natural groups, spontaneous and unforced, into which men necessarily fall. Especially, it appears to me, it is quite too late in the day to draw these lines on points of theological doctrine, —

that is, on points which have and can have no scientific value and no possibility of verification. To a certain extent, those lines will be drawn so naturally. It is not likely that a believer in the Pope's infallibility will seek the sympathy of free religionists; or that a scientific radical would complain of exclusion from a Baptist conference. When the case comes, let it be provided for.

But, in speaking of a communion nominally free, I wish to be understood as meaning all which that term can possibly imply. I take for granted that some serious purpose is meant by voluntarily joining any religious organization at all; and where there is a serious purpose, — even no more than the desire to hear, and perhaps learn, what some new doctrine is, — I hold that no person should have it hinted, or in any way implied, that any difference of opinion from the rest puts him at all in the position of a stranger or outsider, so long as he chooses to stay and claim the sympathy due to a fellow-man. I do not know whether a church, or a religious body, can be built upon so broad a platform; but as liberal men I do not think we have a right to do anything to narrow it, or that as liberal Christians we have a right to exclude, or seem to exclude, any who desire any sort of help, light, or comfort from that source. [1]

I am stating that broad ground of fellowship which

[1] This, evidently, has nothing to do with the question as to the choice or qualifications of a religious teacher, which must be settled not by abstract theory, but by personal considerations and the circumstances of the case.

most Protestant bodies seem to be coming to, consciously or not. In many which call themselves orthodox, all decent people are welcome as members, even as communicants, and no questions asked. But it is desirable that the principle should be distinctly stated and accepted, and not acted on surreptitiously. Especially it is desirable that it should be seen as the natural working-out of opinion, not as if we were driven to it illogically by way of subterfuge. In fact, it is the logical result of the scientific study of theology, which comes in our day to take the place of its dogmatic and controversial study. To see this, it is only necessary to look at the fact before our eyes.

I must add a word here, as to the meaning of the name "Christian," as applied to so loose terms of communion as I have described.

The name was at first, probably enough, used as a term of reproach, or at least simply as the designation of a small party or group of persons at Antioch. The early defenders of Christianity played a good deal upon the word, for as pronounced in Greek it denoted "the party of the good" as well as "the party of Christ."[1] And it has come in course of time to have several meanings, either of which may be true in a particular connection.

It is used in a broad way, historically, to distinguish the Christian world in general from Pagan or Mahometan;

It is used by Catholics, ecclesiastically, to mean those who accept the government, creed, and discipline of the Roman Church;

[1] As derived from χρηστός or from χριστός.

It is used by the Evangelical sects, theologically, to denote those who accept the orthodox scheme of salvation through Christ;

It is used by many religious bodies, technically, to signify those who have been personally converted, and pledged to lead a Christian life;

It is used by Unitarians of the older school, as opposed to deist or rationalist, to describe those who accept the Christian revelation in its strict supernaturalistic sense;

It is used by Unitarians of a newer school to describe those who accept Jesus personally as their authoritative teacher and guide;

It is used by some transcendental thinkers — as it was used with great fervor of insistence by Theodore Parker — in a sense identical with " absolute religion," and by many others, still more loosely, in a sense identical with simple moral goodness;

And, still again, it is used in literature to designate not so much (I should say) virtue in general, but a particular class of moral qualities, sympathies, and aspirations, which it has been the special work of Christianity to foster and educate, — chiefly charity, piety, and chastity, with the qualities that most resemble them, and are of nearest kindred to them.[1]

Thus the name is found, in modern use, in at least eight different senses; and in either one of them, according to the connection, it may be quite rightly used.

---

[1] "It is well understood that, in social parlance, Christianity is a term denuded of all doctrinal signification." — *Saturday Review.*

We notice, besides, that till within the last few years the name Christian was considered rather a privilege, or prerogative, which the most liberal of religious thinkers earnestly claimed as their right, and which ecclesiastics or theologians were just as much inclined to define by sharp boundaries, and to allow or withhold on purely technical grounds. Quite recently, the tide has rather turned the other way. In the increased daring of modern speculation, Christian thinkers, more strictly so called, are inclined to desire and claim the alliance of any who do not choose to take openly antichristian ground. They incline to widen the definition, to level the boundaries, to accept any recruit who will swell their ranks against the "infidelity" of modern science. On the other hand, the more liberal party are not at all anxious about their exclusion from that name, and many of them distinctly repudiate and disclaim it, — some as neutral, others as definitely hostile towards it. To them it is a sectarian name, meaning either narrowness or falsehood according as you look at it; and so, while working out those forms of religious truth in better harmony with the widening range of knowledge and thought, they reject it just as they would any other name of sectarian limitation, or any other antiquated error. [1]

For myself, I am not quite content with either of the definitions I have given. I should state it rather in some such way as this: In religious fellowship

[1] Mr. Emerson, who was understood to have declined the name when it was taken for a theological badge, returned to it, with much affection and veneration, before his death.

our basis of union is not intellectual, or theoretical, but emotional and moral, having to do not with
opinion, but with character and conduct. When I
say that in a given case this is a "Christian" basis
of union, I do not mean to be understood as compromising that statement. The name Christian does
not rest, as I hold it, on any theory whatever about
the nature or office or person or doctrine of Christ.
It rests simply on the fact that we are Christian by
habit or inheritance, unless we deliberately choose to
renounce that name in favor of some other.

Doubtless the name should not be asserted or retained, except so far as it represents the fact. From
the side of free-thought, I am not sure that it always
does; but from the side of associated religious action
it (for the present) very accurately does, in the freest
of our so-called Christian organizations. As distinctly
as I realize any fact in human history, I realize, in
acting with such an organization, that the great Christian movement has not spent its force; but that in
some very important departments of thought, still
more in some of the most vital and practical spheres
of motive and emotion, its current still bears me
along. I yield to its pressure, and consciously work
with it, instead of standing aside to criticise and
judge it independently.

That is what I mean, for my part, by calling
myself a Christian. When I assume that name, I
understand myself not to be professing an article of
belief, however indefinite and vague, but to be stating
an historical fact, definite and precise. Whatever
Christian form or symbol I accept, I understand my-

self not as pledged to any interpretation whatever, which any other man may give or may have given of such form or symbol, but simply as claiming my part in the tradition which has come to us, just as our natural life has, — not by our act or choice, but by drift of circumstance ; and I am entirely free to interpret or use it as I will.

I can well conceive that an interpretation might be forced upon the Christian system or name, by the overwhelming assent of numbers, which would make it personally dishonest and morally impossible for me to retain that name. But at present not only I do not see it in that light, but it is my very business, and the task to which as seeking to interpret a "liberal Christianity " I am most strongly committed, to prevent its being so. For with all its terrible abuses, and with all its pernicious errors, Christianity is a name that means too much for the higher life of men, whether moral or spiritual, to be willingly let die.

It appears to me that, with this explanation of it, neither the name Christian nor the name Unitarian is inconsistent with the most absolute freedom and independence of thought, — understanding, of course, that the thought is in harmony with the main aim and purpose of what we call the Christian life. And this I understand, though not always made quite clear in consciousness, to be the position which the Unitarian body has definitely come to take. I will not press any other illustrations of this which might be given, but will only say that when Dr. Bellows, the most honored and trusted leader of the body, was in control of the " Christian Examiner," its most responsible organ, and I was in confidential relations with him, he, with the noble generosity of nature always characteristic of him, distinctly refused, though at some personal inconvenience and loss, to draw any narrower line of fellowship than what I have attempted to lay down; and as distinctly invited and urged the co-operation of men who, he knew, dissented radically from opinions which to him were sacred and fundamental truth.

The liberalizing of theology has been in some sense the work of Unitarianism from the first. That process includes two distinct steps. One of these steps must be taken by the aid of historical criticism, and the other by the aid of natural science. I say steps, though each of them is a process made up of innumerable steps, and extending over many generations. I have now to give a few words to each: not at all to trace the development of it in past time, but to show, very briefly, the points it has had to meet, and the position it has come to take, in the course of these last few years.

As to historical criticism, few knew even what the phrase meant, not many years before the time I am especially dealing with. Theological polemics was a battle in the air. It was kept up with immense learning on both sides, but with the sole aim on each side to get the victory over the other, and on both, to see which could hit the hardest blows. Each combatant spoke for a party, — evangelical, unitarian, rationalistic, — and his business was to do that party the best service and its adversaries the most damage he could.

This, we know, has been the tone of theological warfare from of old. On the titlepage of his most labored and learned piece of work, the translation of De Wette's "Introduction to the Old Testament," Theodore Parker put the defiant motto, *Strike, but hear.* This motto is strangely out of place in a book of pure erudition ; but it illustrates very well a temper and a method which have not quite passed away. That is the theological method as formerly understood. It is always anticipating hostility, and in a chronic attitude of fighting.

The scientific method is exactly different. It minds its own business of building up what it can, little by little ; and, so long as it minds its business, knows nothing, cares nothing, about any opponents, imaginary or real. The difference, in short, is this : that theology—at least as it was understood once — lays down its plan of thinking, and then goes on with its mode of interpretation in harmony with it ; science builds together its facts, bit by bit, comparing, explaining, investigating, combining, but keeping as clear as may be from all theories whatever, except as they grow irresistibly out of the facts.

In this way it puts together its construction, — not to satisfy a preconceived notion of what must be, but to ascertain as perfectly as it can just what is or was. It knows that our knowledge is imperfect and fragmentary ; that beyond the horizon which we can see are boundless regions which we cannot see. Its work is never to deny what may be beyond, but, by patient exploring, to carry the horizon farther out ; to enlarge the boundaries of accurate knowledge, and within those boundaries to make what we do know more orderly and precise. In this its method is just the reverse of that which theology has more commonly followed. Theology pleads as an advocate; science listens to all the evidence, and holds the balance like a judge.

In saying this, I do not mean that the dogmatic method belongs to the orthodox party in theology, or the scientific to its opponents. I do not observe, for example, that the method of the deists or rationalists is at all more scientific than that it attacked. Hume's, for example, is less so than Lardner's, and Parker's less than Norton's. The difference I wish to point out is between the sober constructive temper on the one side, anxious only to get truth uncolored by prejudice or passion, and the partisan temper on the other side, chiefly anxious to establish a foregone conclusion.

This last has been oftenest shown, no doubt, by theological dogmatists, but often, also, by anti-theological dogmatists. These may be, and often are, generous, large-hearted men, and their work is necessary and noble. Only, they are what they are, and their work is what it is, because for them the day of science is not yet. Metaphysics, destructive dogmatism, anti-theological partisanship, hot passion enlisted against bigotry and intolerance, are necessary to clear the ground. They are the indispensable forerunner, but they are no more what we call science than the theories they oppose. They are simply a protest in the name of intellectual freedom. The zeal and the learning they bring to bear give weight to the protest, and do an infinite service for those who are yet to

follow. But the partisan temper, the breeze of controversy, must lull before we can have a scientific
theology in the proper meaning of that word.

In some respects the present is much more favorable for this than the time that went before. The
controversial temper has abated, and the scientific
temper has had quite a new training in the discussions of these latter years. It would not be correct
to say that interest has lessened in the fundamental
questions of religious thought. It would be more
correct to say that a soberer and more radical, perhaps more anxious, debate is going on as to the religions bearings of natural science as it is now coming
to be understood.   Darwin, Spencer, Tyndall, Huxley,
are names of much more immediate moment to the
theological world than the names of Schleiermacher,
Strauss, Baur, and Parker. In the field of debate
now open, the place of honor is held, not by the
advocates of this or that opinion, but by those who,
patiently, learnedly, and candidly are doing their best
to bring a genuine scientific spirit to bear upon the
facts.

Now, what do we mean by theological science ?
and how do its method and aim differ from those of
physical science ? For example, how does a scientific
theology differ from a scientific physiology ?

The method of natural science is well understood,
which is the observation and comparison of facts ; and
its aim, which is to ascertain the "laws of similitude
and succession" of those facts. Theories of the origin
of life, or the general problem of Being, it dismisses
as belonging altogether to the sphere of the Unknow-

able, or at least as coming under the province not of physics but of metaphysics.

A scientific theology has, to begin with, precisely the same method and aim : it differs only in the data it assumes, and the class of facts with which it has to deal. It has (for example) nothing to do with cosmological theories, evolutionary or other, though many persons seem to suppose so. These, however fascinating or instructive, belong to the field of physical or else metaphysical speculation. The facts it has to do with directly are these : facts of the religious consciousness, and facts of religious history. The laws it has to investigate are the laws of life as they bear on character and conduct. The phenomena it explores are distinctively *religious* phenomena; that is, ethical or emotional. These it is the business of a scientific theology to interpret with as keen an eye to fact, as physiology in interpreting the functions of any organ or tissue. Whether on the narrowest scale in the individual life, or more broadly in the interpretation of sacred literature, or on the largest scale in the great movements of human history, it is the first business of a scientific theology to interpret those facts, or alleged facts, of human life which are remotest from the range of physical necessity, most closely and essentially included in the field of character and will.

Of course, there is a province of pure learning which belongs especially to the theological domain. This includes the vast accumulated erudition in the way of literary criticism, exegesis, dogmatics, historical criticism, and a great proportion of what is commonly reckoned to belong to ecclesiastical history. Some of these topics — ecclesiology and textual criticism, for example — may be even said to constitute special or ancillary sciences in themselves.

So, too, there is a view of the religious life which contemplates its relations with the infinite, the unseen, the incomprehensible ; a view which (in the accepted language of religionists) belongs not to knowledge, but to faith. But for the present, and for the sake of precision, it will be convenient to limit the province of scientific theology to the interpretation of those two classes of facts before designated, — facts of the religious consciousness and facts of religious history.

Just here, and at the very outset, we come upon a wide field of disputed facts, — the so-called supernatural. On the received principles of natural science, what are we to do with these ? Religious history is too full of them to let us pass them by. Our methods of historical criticism are exposed to their sharpest test in dealing with them. We cannot very well begin by assuming that our only witnesses in a given matter are retailing pure falsehood, deceiving or deceived. The mere strangeness of a phenomenon is no logical ground for denying it. Miracles meet us on the threshold of our inquiry ; and one of our first tasks must be to get as clearly before our minds as we can the principles of dealing with them intelligently.

As this is quite the most perplexed and difficult part of our whole inquiry, we must give it a somewhat patient and deliberate attention. Let us begin by noticing one or two contrasts that follow from the difference in the subject-matter between theology and science, as that term is commonly applied.

Science assumes as its postulate or ideal (which it has a perfect right to do), that every group of facts supposably may be, and in time probably will be, reduced within the domain of natural law, — that is, within that orderly succession of events whose antecedents or successions we can intelligently follow, and at length predict; and its objective point will be to reduce as many of them as it can. Theology assumes as its postulate or ideal, that everything at bottom proceeds from living, intelligent, personal force, and sees in any given event an exhibition of that force. It deals, in short, with Persons, as the other deals with Things.

Science has the advantage of showing how a great multitude of facts, once thought to be ultimate (that is to say, super-natural), have been reduced to regular order and succession, grouped and classified, so that the course of them can be predicted or intelligently controlled : storms and eclipses, for example, on one side, and mental maladies on the other, neither of which now seem to us supernatural in origin or subject to miraculous control. Theology has the advantage, as soon as we come to deal with the motives and acts of intelligent beings, and with all the higher manifestations of life, that its theories come closer to our notion of originating force.

Science, again, does not pretend to know anything about the origin of existing things; and, if we attempt to account for that at all, an intelligent Will (as Comte said) is at least as rational and easy a way as any other. Neither has science ever succeeded in reconciling it to the common consciousness of men, that our voluntary acts come within the uniform and necessary sequence of natural law : such words as virtue and crime, right and wrong — belonging in peculiar to the theological domain—always presume the fact of personal responsibility and moral freedom.

In short, we have the two great realms of Law and Will, of necessity and liberty, of natural event and human character, subsisting side by side, and absolutely irreducible either of them to the other. Speaking strictly, a free act is just as much a miracle as the creation of a world ; and, excepting a free act, — that is, an act of intelligent will, such as we are conscious of at any moment, — there is no other miracle.[1]

Now just how far the province of will, human or divine, extends in the field of action or history, it is not for any man to dogmatize. Most of us would admit that an intelligent act was required, at any rate, to start the human race on its course, and to appoint the Law which has guided its evolution. To some of us — and perhaps more and more, the more we reflect upon it — it will appear not unlikely that a living influence, a pressure (so to speak) like that of the atmosphere, is felt in human affairs, acting everywhere and always, but especially through minds of certain peculiar capacities and gifts ; and that this influence (which must be allowed for just as we allow for the pressure of the atmosphere in mechanics) is

[1] The point is further developed in Dr. Bushnell's " Nature and the Supernatural."

from a sphere outside the will, or the conscious intelligence of men. It is not a thing to dogmatize about; and its laws, supposing it to work by law, do not seem very likely to come within the range of our mental science. Still, in speaking of it, we should bear in mind that we are speaking of nothing contra-natural or abnormal, but of what comes into the same order of fact as the evolution of a planet or the simplest act of volition.

Here, then, is the point to which we are led. All that we call miraculous and supernatural, the whole province of revelation and inspiration, lies (as all history does) in this field, which belongs alike to science and to theology: to one as the exponent of Law, and to the other as the asserter of Will. The question between them is simply how far the province of will, or personal force, can enter upon and control the domain of law, or natural sequence. If we say never and not at all, we assert a mere dogmatic fatalism, which is not only incapable of proof, but is in violent contradiction to our moral consciousness. If we say it may enter, ever so little way, by the original act of the Creator, or by the free lifting of a hand, then we waive all dogmatic *a priori* denial of the possibility of miracle and revelation;[1] and it only remains to us to inquire, as accurately as we can, what is the real fact covered by those words.

But that is not going to prove, as some theologians have imagined, a short and easy process. It will not do to take a single style of mental illumination, and

---

[1] Obviously a different thing from the legitimate logical presumption against marvels.

a single group of acts, appearing at one given period of history, and say that all revelation and miracle are included here. Still less will it do to accept off-hand one class or school of evidences as to these particular facts, and rule out off-hand all other evidence as to similar facts appearing at other times and in other ways. The records of history are full of alleged miracles, oracles, wonders, presumed to be supernatural. If the Hebrew and Christian records make a class entirely by themselves, and are to stand alone in all the world as sufficient evidence of revelation and miracle (which, with many, is the only point at issue), that fact itself cannot be established without exhaustive criticism and comparison, and a long and intricate process of study, which is hardly more than begun.

Grant that in these two groups of records there are characteristics quite unique, giving them a claim to be valued and studied quite peculiar to them, and shared by no other, — and there is a good deal in them to justify that claim, — still this by no means forestalls the duty, in the face of the immense learning and argument arrayed against it, of establishing it patiently and good temperedly, by fair reasoning ; not asserting it violently, on peril of denunciation or worse, or even assuming it in advance to be defended afterwards. Suppose those records to be intrinsically and exceptionally divine, it will be some generations yet before that fact can be sufficiently established to serve for a valid theory of sacred history. The old proofs of it served for a time, but the whole process of proof has now to abide a different class of tests.

Two needless difficulties have been introduced here by modern defenders of miracles.

The first is the view which sees in them manifestations, or invasions, of a higher realm of Law, overriding and controlling those lower ranges of law with which we are familiar. This needless concession to the terminology of science is dispensed with, by taking the simpler definition of a miracle, as an act of Will under conditions exceptional and imperfectly understood, particularly when those conditions have to do with man's nervous or psychical organization. The *conditions*, here as elsewhere, are defined by law ; but the *act of will* is in its nature (so far as it reaches) the overruling of law. What is Law, after all, except *an observed sequence of phenomena?* If there is any force behind it, that is quite as likely to be intelligent and free as otherwise.

The other difficulty is the assumption, often silently made, that the exception which makes the miracle is to be allowed in a single class of miracles only, — those of the Bible, which are involved in a particular theological scheme. Thus the hardest and most disputed point in the problem is put in front, to be met first. It is evident, on the contrary, that the true method would be to take the easiest and nearest first, — to decide, if possible, on the alleged miracles of our own time ; to examine testimony from other parts of the historical field ; and thus to secure in advance the canons of evidence by which the miracles of Scripture may be brought under scientific tests.

I will not speak here of the great field that is

opened by the study of comparative religions, but only of what belongs directly to the history and development of Christianity itself. Its earliest defenders (as Justin) admitted the reality of pagan oracles and miracles, which they ascribed to evil dæmons, while they laid no claim to supernatural powers of their own. Its later advocates — conspicuously Augustine and Gregory of Tours — testify in the most detailed and explicit way to miracles of healing and of raising from the dead, in their own experience, and by powers directly conferred on Christian believers. The testimony of these dignified and important eye-witnesses is very different from the innumerable miraculous legends that swarm in ecclesiastical chronicles and lives of the saints.

Catholic believers, however, have always asserted that their Church retained its wonder-working power. Some years ago, when living in Washington, I was informed in great detail of a church miracle of healing which had been wrought there very recently, with all formality and publicity. Sometimes tales like these vanish when you come near them; sometimes they do not. And no evidence in history appears to be plainer, more explicit, or more respectable, than what comes to us daily of works of healing, or the like, quite outside any known scientific method, which can be ascribed only to the exertion of the will under special conditions: that is, they come under any definition of miracle which can be intelligently framed. All these make part of the field open to scientific exploration.

I do not bring up these illustrations as an argument bearing one way or the other on the reality of miraculous phenomena. Personally, I have no theoretical objection whatever to what are commonly called miracles, in the only sense in which I can understand that term, — that is, as acts of will, whether human or divine, under conditions which have not yet been, and perhaps never will be, reduced within our science. What I do object to is the logical inconsistency of applying canons of evidence to one set of facts, which we refuse at the same time to apply to another set of facts.

I do not say, either, that all those facts must stand or fall together. They are found in great variety, and supported by widely different degrees of proof. I do not even deny that the final result of the most skilful and fair investigation may be to leave the miracles of the Bible in their place of honor, the sole and only facts of that order which history will allow permanently to stand. I only say that the preliminary studies have not yet been undertaken, — at least, not carried by any means far enough, — to justify that as the final verdict. Men of science have been too radically hostile to the very idea of miracle, or in fact of any free-agency at all; while theologians have been too tenaciously bent on proving or disproving the authenticity of particular books, to allow the real question to come before the court of reason.

For the present, therefore, what we are entitled to demand is this: that the Biblical record, after due process of literary criticism, shall be judged exactly as we judge other records, ancient or modern, of alleged contemporary fact. More than this the friends of science have no right to demand; less than this they cannot be asked or expected to accept.

I say nothing of what it may be when the true conditions of historical criticism are better understood. But provisionally, and for the present, we seem to be justified in accepting a Scripture miracle as true, if the same or a corresponding degree of evidence would convince us of the same thing happening in Asia to-day or in America a hundred years ago; and we are not justified in so accepting it if the same or a corresponding degree of evidence would not convince us of the same thing happening in Asia to-day or in America a hundred years ago. And at all events we need, to establish our canons of evidence or our test of credibility, some well certified and generally accepted judgment of scientific men, after sufficient investigation, of the alleged " miracles " of our own day. No other judgment appears to be either rational, adequate, or candid.

Accepting this as a general criterion, we shall not, probably, be over hasty or confident in applying it to the record of particular facts. If, however, we may judge by the turn given to modern observation of such things, it would appear that there is one large class of Scripture miracles, or what are generally regarded as such, — chiefly the healing of nervous and mental disorders, — which we may accept with little hesitation, subject, of course, to the criticism of an improved physiology. There are others — chiefly those concerning certain natural phenomena — which we should almost certainly reject as facts, without any hesitation at all. Some of them may be poetry, like that of Joshua and the sun; some allegory or myth, like that of Jonah and the whale, the ascension of Elijah, or the children in the fiery furnace; some — like the feeding of the multitudes, stilling the tempest, walking on the waves, or blasting the fig-tree — a natural enough misunderstanding of the real fact (whatever that may have been), or perhaps a parable misconceived. Such expositions lie mostly in the region of pure hypothesis.

There are others which have taken a deeper hold on the religious imagination, and which have become, so to speak, articles of religious faith in themselves. As to these, the judgment of candid and honest minds is likely to be greatly in suspense, and painfully. That we cannot help. We wish to see, if we are candid and honest, just where our principles of belief are likely to lead us.

Of such events the typical one, and beyond comparison the most momentous, is the resurrection of Jesus. To this our ordinary canons do not quite apply: first, because absolute belief in it, by those who claimed to be eye-witnesses, was the mainspring of a great and definite movement in human history; and second, because belief in it not only qualifies men's view of the course of events in general (as all miracle does), but is apt to determine their whole view of human life and destiny. Not only as the demonstration of a life to come, but as symbol and proof of the victory of good over evil, the place which it holds in the religious mind is entirely unique. Criticism is therefore bound to approach it more deliberately, more anxiously, more tenderly, than it approaches any other which it is really seeking to understand.

We may admit, at the outset, the overwhelming presumption which the modern mind finds against the literal interpretation of the narrative. It is probably not too much to say that no educated mind — that is, no mind trained in modern methods — now believes that a body of flesh and blood literally came from the grave, and in plain sight of men rose above the clouds, — the view of it which most early believers maintained with great intrepidity. That has passed away, along with the dogma of the resurrection of the body, which it was held to prove.

The alternative which forces itself upon the modern mind is plain: either there was no real death, or there was no real revival of the dead. No weight of evidence will outweigh the vast improbability. But that alternative only brings us to the threshold of the interpretation we seek. It only puts the question in another form: Is it possible for a human soul, after death, to manifest its presence in a way of which the resurrection of Jesus is an example and a type? And to this question there are several affirmative answers, giving as many phases of belief, — none of them disproved, and some of them, it may be, not incapable of future proof.

A *valid* answer, again, would give — or for it we should need — a far better knowledge than we have now of the exact relation between this and what, for want of better knowledge, we call the unseen world. Granting only that such a realm of conscious life exists, it would be absurd to deny that it could be made known to us; and there would remain no difficulty either in the recorded appearances of Jesus, or in countless other manifestations of spirits that have passed into it before us. It becomes simply a question of the larger possibilities and destinies of human nature.

It is perfectly easy to see what the first disciples understood by the resurrection of Jesus, and in what sense they believed in it. Paul, to be sure, the earliest Christian writer, speaks of it very vaguely, except as to the point of its reality, which he insists on in every possible way, as the very foundation of Christian faith. This reality,' to his mind, is the glorified life in heaven of the living and exalted Messiah, who, in his new official station, is the direct source of inspiration and strength to his disciples. The particular event and way of "the resurrection from the dead" he says nothing about, except to insist that it is *not* a form of flesh and blood, but a "spiritual body," that dwells in the after-life.

But the next generation have left us no room whatever to doubt of their meaning. They have explained and argued, in the most explicit terms, that it *was* a body of flesh and blood which rose from the grave. It was proved to be so by the act of eating and drinking; it was shown by wounds and scars to be the same that was actually mangled upon the cross; and it was visibly taken up in plain daylight into the sky. It is saying nothing whatever to criticise or condemn that belief, to say that it has passed wholly out of the educated mind of the present day, along with the kindred and dependent doctrine of the resurrection of our **own bodies.**

Of modern expositions, accepted by Unitarians, may be mentioned the following: —

Dr. Furness sets aside the whole accompaniment of angelic visions, and represents Jesus as rousing himself as if from a deep sleep, — manifestly implying that there had been no death in the ordinary or physiological sense.

Mr. Edmund H. Sears — a mind rare and admirable, in whom piety and imagination were matched by equal literary vigor and charm — held that the risen body of Jesus became by degrees, during forty days, attenuated, spiritualized, visionary, so attaining the condition of what is called the " resurrection body," in which condition it was withdrawn from human sight.[1]

James Freeman Clarke regards the resurrection of Jesus as " an example of a universal law," and his visible appearances as illustrating the conditions under which the departed may manifest themselves in a " spiritual body," — his real body having been removed by priests or soldiers.[2] We have here, apparently, the same phenomenon as in the " materializations " of modern Spiritism; since " a universal law" cannot, of course, be inferred from a single disputed example.

President Walker — one of the most grave, candid, and honored of Unitarian thinkers — held, more simply, that the resurrection of Jesus was really the

---

[1] Foregleams of Immortality.
[2] Orthodoxy, its Truths and Errors, p. 83.

strong personal impression or conviction of his living presence, produced on the minds of his disciples by his own spiritual contact and influence while in the unseen world, which they interpreted as a visible appearance. To him the Ascension was decisive against a material resurrection.

A view to which many of the most thoughtful and intelligent appear to incline — most strikingly set forth by the author of " Philochristus " — is, that the imagination and faith of the disciples created outright those visions or appearings of their risen Lord which afterwards took shape in the gospel narratives, or in later legends, — hard to reconcile with one another, but easy to reconcile by that vivid and creative fancy, inspired by revering affection, and an absolute hope of his future return in celestial glory.

These are interpretations suggested by believing, serious, religious minds. Mere scientific criticism, neutral or hostile, goes much further, so as to make the whole account sheer fabrication, imposture, myth, or hallucination.

I have thus indicated what appears to me the true attitude of scientific thought towards the most disputed and difficult questions of theology, in which I do not include such properly philosophical or metaphysical questions as the being or attributes of God, freedom of the will, and the natural argument for immortality. For the profoundest thought on these questions of the higher philosophy, from the Unitarian point of view, I may refer to Dr. Hedge's " Reason in Religion," and " Ways of the Spirit," or to the superb and eloquent exposition that has been given of these and similar topics by Mr. James Martineau.

I have been drawn into making this discussion, more than I meant, a statement of personal opinion as far as it goes; because that seems fairer than a method purely impersonal and non-committal. It appears to me that the chief lesson we have to learn as to these matters is modesty and patience. Hasty dogmatism is the demand of the impatient partisan, and the source of never-ending, bitter, fruitless controversy. What I have called a "scientific" method of dealing with the subject will tolerate no such thing. The long experience of physical investigation, leading to the enormous enlargement of our positive knowledge and power, teaches always this one lesson, — intellectual humility.

Science forbids partisanship and passion: it does not forbid an intense, deep, personal interest in the wide field it explores. The world of man — of emotion, character, and act opened to us in Christian history and in the study of the human soul — is far nearer to our thought, and far more interesting, than the splendid realm of outward phenomena taught in our cosmology and our physics. Let it be studied with equal patience, reverence, humility, with equal loyalty to the revelation of simple fact, and its fruit will not be less precious or abundant.

Again: Science involves Criticism; and the results of criticism are often, for the time at least, negative, not positive. But while there is many a thing which we can only have left behind with reluctance and pain, yet as one is intellectually the "heir of all the ages," so the later he inherits, the richer his inheritance. The scientific spirit is likely to prove braver, manlier, honester, than the ecclesiastical spirit, even if less serious and tender; and the tendency to a certain mental timidity, half-heartedness, and compromise can never again, I should think, be quite as strong as some of us have felt it in the past.

There is always a temptation to try our hand at some ideal theory of reconciliation and mental harmony among the widely diverse elements of our experience. But history makes very light of all such ideal theories. We are not responsible for the beginning of things, or for the end of things; though by a sort of generous illusion we are apt to feel so. For us, the only answer of any value to any of the great questions respecting God, Life, Destiny, is the answer we find — very slowly and late in life perhaps — by doing our own best work in our own best way; and in keeping mind and heart always open to the whisper of the Spirit of all Truth. And that is, after all, the best contribution we can make to the larger result,— perhaps the only one.

VII.

THE RELIGION OF HUMANITY.

THAT very brilliant and striking book, "Ecce Homo," has made familiar the phrase "enthusiasm of humanity," to describe the spirit which, more than anything else, characterized the new religion as it was conceived in the minds of Jesus and his disciples.

This may be justified, perhaps, by the emphasis which the New Testament lays on the purely human qualities of justice, charity, and compassion, above all tradition, form, or doctrine. And there was a time when the Christian Church assumed the heaviest of tasks in the preserving or reconstructing of society in a long period of violence and disorder. That was, however, in the name of God, not man, and by the offices of a priest, not by appealing broadly to the human reason ; still less by the intelligent study of the causes that make for human welfare and virtue as against misery and crime.

Thus the phrase "enthusiasm of humanity" was never properly characteristic of the Christian Church as such; and it never had a distinct meaning in anybody's mind till within the last hundred years. It really belongs not to the religion of the past, but to the religion of the future. And when we speak of any connection it may have with the liberal movement in theology, we speak of the most important thing of all, in which that may have any hold upon, or any service of preparation for, or any hope in, that better life for man at which Religion aims.

Here let me recall a single step of the ground over which we have already passed. Unitarianism, as it was at the end of the last century, had in it two elements: the element of Reason, in which it was an outgrowth of the realistic school of Locke; and the element of Justice, in which it was allied with the revolutionary spirit and the political radicalism of a hundred years ago.

In its later history in this country these two elements have continually reappeared side by side. They have determined, on the one hand, the movement of free-thought against the old theology, and, on the other hand, they have defined the issues of later controversy. Let us see to what point they have already brought us.

It may be fairly said that reason is now in the ascendant in the field of theology. The old questions of history, criticism, and dogma are, it is true, far enough from being settled; but at least they have all been brought under a scientific method of inquiry, which (so far as we can see) is their final stage. But thought is, at best, an inconsiderable part of the domain of life. If the next great development of religion is to be in the direction of intelligent service of humanity, — which, with all generous minds, is to take the place of ritual and dogma, — our most important study must be the antecedents, principles, and conditions of that service.

The Christian ideal of human society is summed up in the phrase, "Kingdom of heaven upon earth." In its practical sense, that ideal was soon in great part lost sight of by the early Church. The old creed, Catholic and Calvinist alike, had its root in a sort of despair of human nature and earthly destiny. In strong contrast to the New Testament, it remanded to a future paradise and hell the solution of a riddle which (as we see with Saint Augustine) it felt itself incompetent to solve in this world.

The great reaction against that creed began with the deism and philosophism of the last century. The gross sins of Voltaire, the grosser offences of Rousseau, against general faith and morals, are more than atoned, in the view of our generation, by the intrepid humanity of the one and the sentimental pleadings of the other. This new spirit, still fresh, vivid, and full of hope, inspired the era and dictated the maxims of the Revolution. It is just over a hundred years since the new gospel of humanity, the modern creed of liberty and equal right, was put in distinct expression to justify our declaration of national independence, to inspire enthusiasm in a doubtful struggle, and to assert the principles of a new political life. In France, what we should call the modern Bill of Rights is still appealed to as the "idea of eighty-nine;" that is, it defines the doctrine and aim of the Revolution as against the old constitution of State and Church.

This new gospel of humanity, the code of human rights, became a sort of religion in its way, and the object of as passionate devotion as any religious dogma of the past. Theophilanthropy — as it was called in one of those fervid episodes — under the banner of "that good democrat Jesus," or of the new revolutionary "Supreme," was an attempt to enlist the impassioned enthusiasm of the religious sentiment in the war against privilege and wrong. Its doctrine was futile, its forms were melodramatic and ridiculous. But, as far as sentiment goes, nothing was ever more generous ; few things, I should think, have been more sincere. A humble but very touching illustration of it struck my eye in visiting the great School of the Blind, in Paris, where the dates of charitable foundations and gifts were the dates of successive stages in the French Revolution ; and recalled not the eras' of prosperity and glory, not the splendors of aristocracy and court, but the time of terror, when the people felt the first sense of a blood-bought power, and France was in arms against the world.

Now from that period of revolution our own has grown, and has received no small part of its spiritual inheritance. And especially among us here in America. Here, that sentiment of justice and equal right has been cultivated, for more than a century, as a sort of religion. It has been proclaimed in innumerable patriotic addresses, and sung in all our national songs, and incorporated as a bill of rights in our State constitutions, and made the only basis of political power. Even now, the enormous inconvenience of irresponsible suffrage and sentimental legislation has hardly begun to check the fervor of that early faith. In the most formidable political crisis we have met, the sentiment of equal liberty, as much as the plain necessity of national union, was the condition and the assurance of our victory.

What made the religion of our politics inspired also the reform of our religion. When the revolutionary gospel of humanity had become so deeply discredited abroad, when the *Te Deum* of the Holy Alliance had been chanted over its downfall, then it became part of the task of Christian liberalism to give what was true in it a fresh consecration, and baptize it anew in the name of the Son of Man.

Nothing is more characteristic of the early Unitarianism than this: that, in proportion as it departed from the old theology, and especially as its moral doctrine was more clearly contrasted with the creed of inherited depravity, it became committed to a generous faith in human nature, and more and more made its religion consist in service to mankind.

Thus the doctrine of peace was fervently proclaimed, with strong abhorrence of all war, — a part of the reaction which set in after the five-and-twenty years of carnage that ceased at Waterloo. The temperance reform in its first stages was part of the same generous gospel, and found nowhere else so forward advocates as in the ranks of the liberal theology. The great expansion given to the prevalent ideas of education, and the great improvements in its method which came in forty or fifty years ago, had no more zealous propagandists. When public attention was turned to asylums for the blind, and hospitals for the insane, and reformatories for young offenders, and humane methods of prison discipline, — all these were taken up, in an eager, hopeful way, and engrafted on the same humanitarian creed. That genial optimism, that faith of sentiment, that buoyant confidence in a golden future just opening, when all the harsher wrongs that afflict humanity should melt before the rising of that auspicious sun, — this made part of the atmosphere of liberal theology of forty years ago, and deeply tinged the light under which its younger disciples then looked forward to their life-work as it lay before them.

I must now speak of a certain reaction in the years that have followed since. For two distinct results may be traced as succeeding that era of fervid proclamation and humanitarian faith. The first is, that the faith itself has been cheapened (as it were) by diffusion, and takes the form of that shallow sentimentalism which is one definite source of mischief in the social theories of the day; the second is the shape which the reaction is apt to take with those who have outgrown its crude but ingenuous fervor. A weak humanitarianism on one side is matched against a sombre pessimism on the other.

Those axioms of political justice, those maxims of social ethics, which make the human side of our religious creed, are each a half-truth touching some fact of human nature: the bright or illuminated side, but not the whole of it. To state it as if it were the whole truth makes one of the most troublesome of those fallacies with which morals or politics has to deal. A fallacy of this sort is sometimes a rudimentary or embryonic truth, sometimes a stranded or fossil truth. What is the inspiration of one age may be the delusion of the next. What is the illumination of one period may be the *ignis fatuus* of another. In a high flood-tide of sentiment, action becomes heroic, which when the tide goes down becomes impossible or else insane : witness the Crusades, — a genuine enthusiasm of pious adventure, under Godfrey or St. Bernard ; a dreary and languid tragedy, under Simon Montfort or the contemporaries of St. Louis. At the same flood-tide, a belief becomes passionate and fervent, a hero's inspiration or a martyr's strength, which fades out afterwards into a symbol, an opinion, a creed, with the divine life all ebbed away. So it was with the trinity, with transubstantiation, with the infallibility of the Bible ; so it is with that sentiment of a Divine Humanity, which perpetually tends to fade into the thin cold light of sentimentalism.

There is something ungracious in appearing to disown thus the popular gospel of our time, — so generous in its sympathy, so gushing in its philanthropy, so zealous in its works of charity, so honorable to human nature itself as compared with the creed of any former generation, so congenial to our own best tradition and theory of Christianity. But we cannot fail to see that the waters are ebbing away, on which it floated so fair and brave a generation or two ago. Men's faith in human nature is undergoing a stern revision, and collation with pitiless facts. What is already part of our tradition — what is taken for granted in easy assent, not fought out and won in the mind's own effort after truth and the soul's hunger after righteousness — is no longer the same thing. It is beginning already to be debased and alloyed. The same gospel of humanity which Channing made the most advanced interpretation of Christianity in his day, was greeted with eager welcome as the soul of a new thing in literature when Dickens took his heroes from the work-house and his heroines from the street. Even then there was something in it melodramatic and false. The same thing, at a later stage, becomes conscious satire thinly disguised, as in " Joshua Davidson " and " Ginx's Baby." Striking at very obvious social wrongs, it suggests no solution, unless it be socialism or a spurious Romanism,—as in the wretched sophisms and travesties of Mr. Mallock.

Meanwhile, since the Dickens period, — the period of a gushing and morbid sentimentalism, — literature has taken quite another phase. It has become critical, cynic, weary. Just as theology becomes erudition, as philosophy turns into formula, and science into sterile nomenclature, so in the arts of culture mental analysis goes back on enthusiasm and faith. This tone, not lacking in George Eliot, strongly colors the atmosphere in which the facts of life and history are set before the sight of a younger generation.

So far as we are conscious of it in our own mood, we might suspect it to be the loss of the natural glow of youth as years go by, an outgrowing of the emotions and aspirations of our own past. But it is more than that. In the generation that comes after ours it is still more marked than it is in us. The younger culture has already outgrown, or else has never shared, the generous illusions which made our own inheritance from the Revolutionary age. I speak here more especially of the cultured, the literary, the scientific class. In the popular mind, less touched by the critical temper of the time, those vague emotions, those generous maxims, retain more force. But from the inspiration of a reforming zeal they become dogmas of a sentimentalizing policy. From glittering generalities on the banner in front of battle they degenerate to mere fallacies of social ethics, languid half-truths, whose side of truth, even, is not recognized by those who think they have outgrown them.

For facts, alas! have not borne out those generous vaticinations. For the first time in the world, a whole people were trusted to exhibit the doctrine of equal rights in the government of a Free State, — to issue in the present condition of our politics. We fondly hoped, we fervently believed, that the reign of force was passing away before the advance of reason and humanity; but, behold! six great wars crowded within five and twenty years (to omit such tragic episodes as India and Mexico), — wars engaging the most advanced and powerful Christian nations, and each in its way memorable for some new horror, on some vaster scale than all the tragedies of the past had quite prepared us for! Nations and laws, we said, are shaped more and more by the spirit of Christian philanthropy. But, no! Blood and iron, says the foremost statesman of the age, — blood and iron make the strong cement in which the foundations of States must be laid. And perhaps in all human history the secret dread of war was never so deeply felt as now, and the open preparations for war were never half so formidable.

Was, then, that faith in human nature which made the most choice and precious part of our religious inheritance, — that which seemed benign and sure as sunlight to our fathers, — was it a delusion and a dream ? Such questions many ask themselves in a sort of despair. The answer can come only in a working faith, too busy in act to speculate on result; or else in an intellectual faith, which must grow up slowly among the new conditions of the time. It is quite too soon to do more than guess and hint what the new gospel of humanity shall be. Despair is for the idle and unfaithful, hope for the willing and strong.

Let us now consider briefly the background which is given us for the new Religion of Humanity in the scientific conceptions of the day.

First of all, I do not think we need trouble ourselves in the least about the effect of natural science upon our speculative theism. The God of scientific theory by no means appeals to devout feeling, like the Divine Father of the Christian gospel, but is at least as good as the subjective Absolute of metaphysics, and infinitely better than the avenging Sovereign of the popular theology. And by the God of scientific theory I mean simply the Force — personal or impersonal — behind all phenomena, with which science, as such, has nothing to do; which it knows only as manifest in the primary qualities of matter and the laws of motion. The mystery of the universe itself is so prodigious that it makes light of all our little differences in the attempt to state it.

Consider, for example, what the most bigoted ma-

terialist must embrace in his summary of facts. He
believes, — such is his reliance on the veracity of
things, — with absolute conviction, that in spaces
immeasurably remote he has ascertained the presence
of vast nebulæ of substances having the exact prop-
erties of elements familiar to his experiments; that
there as here, at a given temperature, a given pair of
them (as oxygen and hydrogen) will infallibly unite,
always and everywhere in proportions exactly fixed,
with accuracy more perfect than any chemist's balance could weigh them out; that the vapor thence
resulting will just as infallibly, at a given lower temperature, crystallize in myriads of frosty stars, with
every angle measured by a geometry more exquisite
than any human draughtsman's, — the effect if not
the act of perfect Intelligence, most literally present
in every spot, in every atom. And this, only one of
the simplest of innumerable chemical changes best
known to us; a rude intermediate process, we may
even call it. WHAT MAKES IT ? Answer that, and
you have answered everything. A single one of
Helmholtz's whirling rings (which make the ultimate
form of molecule as now conceived by many) is a
creation as astonishing as a solar system. Account
for that, and you have accounted for everything.

When the same process of unfailing accuracy is
traced through increasing complications of being, up
to all forms of organic growth, without a single loop-
hole left anywhere for chance or caprice, — absolute
Intelligence seen everywhere in result, if not in act,
— it seems a very harmless thing, after all, to say
that Matter, so regarded, has in it "the potency and

the promise of all forms of life." And that "harp of three thousand strings," which Tyndall describes as existing in the structure of the human ear, shaped by the needs and cravings of the organization so as to respond to every tone or finest interval of musical sound, — well! if these are the responses and the potencies existing among material things, I do not know where we could possibly go for a definition of Creative Intelligence, infallible, omnipresent, absolute, so well as to the repertory in which a thorough-going materialist keeps his store of facts; or to that curious summary of them in which Hartmann records the attributes of "The Unconscious." Special arguments of efficient or final cause seem dwarfed into nothingness beside the simple statement of the fact. They testify, at best, to the thoughtful and reverent habit of the mind which contemplates the fact.

Scientific theory, then, I think, is absolutely neutral as to our speculative theism, serving only (as it necessarily must) to state the conditions under which it must be held. But it is a very different thing as it affects our *religious* theism. When we think of the overwhelming vastness, the appalling indifference to our interests and emotions, to all human pain and guilt, with which the circles of Being sweep their everlasting round, can we, — that is, under the ordinary limitations of the human mind, — can we think of any conscious sympathy between our own life and that stupendous Force? Can we conceive or retain a belief that events are intelligently ordered, to work out the designs of "the highest Wisdom and the primal Love"? Dante could dare to put those words on the portal of his Hell, because the system of things he knew of was so small and near. Can we still hold them true, as a key to the inmost meaning of our Cosmos, so vast and with a horizon so remote?

In trying to see how this question may possibly show itself to the modern mind, outside of theological circles, one or two considerations occur. I put that question once to Louis Agassiz; and while he very earnestly urged the proof of Intelligent Design in the creation, it seemed to me that he did not find in nature any very clear mark of the *character* of the Creator, — the only point which has any other than a purely speculative interest for us. And, on the speculative side, the answer given by most interpreters of science is simply negative. The being and character of God are topics with which, as such, it would appear that science has nothing whatever to do.

Now it is not easy for us, who are trained to a very keen interest in primal and final causes, to understand this attitude of absolute intellectual indifference or reserve. The Positive philosophy — or by whatever other name we call the general view of things taken by the scientific mind — by no means attempts so foolish and hopeless a task as to *account* for the existence of anything by those laws of phenomena with which alone it professes to deal. Mr. Martineau's very eloquent and noble essay disclaims any purpose of arguing with any form of Materialism which does not show on its own principles a solution to the problem of existence. Now no recognized form of Materialism at the present day, surely, attempts any such thing. "But," said a friend to Professor Tyndall,

"surely you must have some theory of the Universe."
"My dear sir," was the reply, "I have not even a
theory of Magnetism."

This mood of mind is not necessarily either irreligious or atheistical. We do not, as a general rule,
experience an access of religious emotion when we
light the gas with a match, although the process is as
much more intricate and curious as it is more convenient than the spindle and stick which our ancestors
held sacred for thousands of years, because that was
the way the miracle of fire had come to them. Yet
we do not hold ourselves more undevout than they.
"I am no atheist," Comte protested vehemently: he
said it to me about two years before his death. An
atheistic theory of the universe he held to be the
mere dotage of metaphysical vanity. If you will
have a theory of existence, he said, an Intelligent
Will is the best you can have.[1] In his unique fashion, he held it the great work of his life to restore to
Religion its supremacy in all matters of conduct; the
very phrase "religion of humanity" is claimed as his
invention. But all theories of theology, cosmogony,
metaphysics, and sidereal astronomy were ruled off
with impartial rigor from his intellectual scheme, as
they were from his notion of the service of Humanity
in a working world.

And, again, it is not easy for us, dealing as we do
with human life very much on its emotional side, in
view of its deeper consolations and nobler hopes, to

---

[1] "However imperfect the natural order, its origin would agree
far better with the supposition of an Intelligent Will than with
that of blind Mechanism." — *Politique Positive*, vol. i. p. 51.

conceive the condition of mental calm with which it may be looked on by those who think of these as of the dreams of children. What consolation, we think, for those who do not accept life as the discipline of a Father? What hope to those who anticipate nothing beyond the sensible horizon that bounds our days?

Questions such as these we are apt to argue with a certain sense of personal responsibility for the result, —as if the reality of a life beyond turned on our own power to make it real to our own thought; as if one forfeited his immortality by being unable to believe in it; as if it were impossible for another to win calmness of mind on any other terms than ours. Yet, as matter of history, we know that Spinoza was singularly calm and pure in his submissive sense of the Universal Order; as matter of fact, we know that life does not lose its keen interest, intellectual or other, for those who deliberately rule out from their scheme of things all "thoughts that wander through eternity." I have heard that, in a convention of seven hundred European scientists, not one admitted the thought of personal immortality as possible. Yet the daily work of science, done by a thousand hands, is as diligent, as devoted, in its way quite as contented with itself, as the daily work of ecclesiastics and devotees.

But there is a certain spirit and temper, not essentially connected with natural science, and making no part of its creed, which yet claims close affinity with it. And this spirit or temper tends more and more to show itself not simply neutral, not merely contemptuously indifferent, but definitely hostile — not to this or that creed or form of Christianity, not to the mere name of it, but to ideas and emotions that have always been held to belong to its inmost life. Thus that circle of Christian ideas included in the words *sin, repentance, pardon, atonement, salvation, holiness* — which we have ourselves been at so much pains to interpret in our reading of the religious life — is, as I understand it, radically opposed by the general view of life widely coming to prevail. As far as it does prevail, those words will have not merely to be explained, but to be explained away. This hostility, in so far as it does exist, we ought — as theologians, still more as religious men — to look in the face, and understand it if we can.

At the outset, the theory of Evolution itself is a great shock to the feeling of the sacredness of human life, so carefully cherished by Christianity; and to the sense of the dignity of human nature, which marked our earlier interpretation of Christianity. The shock will pass away in time, and the religious feeling will get adjusted to the new surroundings. But let us do justice to the deep repugnance with which that theory has been resented. That the mythical first human pair — with its halo of marvel and reverence, with the schemes of history and theology grouped about it — should be displaced by the chance coupling of a superior breed of "anthropoid apes" stronger and cunninger than the rest, with lower forms of bestiality in the background; or, if not this, yet the wild and brutish savagery of the primitive man, out of which the race has fought its way to something better, through perhaps a thousand centuries' struggle for existence, — all this may be the best way we have at present of stating the facts; but, after all, the facts are not pleasant to look at so, and we have not got used to looking at them yet, in that shape, from the religious point of view. Our debt to the Humanity that has suffered and toiled before us is even enhanced by that statement, as has been well said; but somehow the Divine guiding Hand is not, to the common eye, so plain to see.

And so, again, when we first clearly foresaw the doom that awaits, at however distant date, all forms of life upon this planet; when we learned that we could no longer look forward to an indefinite career of progress for the human race upon earth, but, as the wave of life has risen, so it must inevitably subside; when we saw, too, that civilization itself is a destructive as well as a creative process, and that the treasures we thought exhaustless may be economized, but must be spent, — it was with a sort of chill. What are four or five thousand years, what are two hundred thousand (plausibly enough reckoned as the limit of past and future duration to the human race), in comparison with eternity? The destined end of all things and systems visible to us is announced by Science with a certain pitiless precision; and no compensation is even suggested for the enormous presumption that is asserted to lie against our hope of personal immortality. If human life in its origin looks ignoble, under the light of modern theory, even more depressing is the aspect, so regarded, of its destiny and end.

Now this, unwelcome as it may be to our religious feeling, is distinctly the order of conceptions and ideas which the religious thinker of our time has got to meet. For the present, apart from religious feeling, it appears to have had two distinct effects on men's imagination. The first is a certain hard, unsympathetic way of regarding human life on a large scale, — history merging into anthropology, and that more and more into natural history, especially when it deals with the lower races or classes of mankind, and so emerging in great disdain and race or class pride among the superior. " We will not be missionaries any more," it says, " and sacrifice ourselves for the barbarian. Let the perishing classes go. It is the law of the struggle for existence that they should perish and make place for those worthier to live than they," — that is, ourselves. The other effect is a certain dreary and sad way of seeing things, as if the vast tragedy of human life were vulgarized, from the terror and the pity (which make it *human* tragedy) being taken out of it, seen from the austere height of modern speculation.

This double tendency, to aristocratic pride on the one side and a sombre pessimism on the other, I do not think can be denied to be a very common and formidable symptom in the educated mind of the day. If any one were to doubt it, I should ask him to consider the tone of Strauss's retrospect, the pyramid-like ethnology of Renan, the dreary view of nature and life that impressed itself on the keen susceptibility of John Stuart Mill, the deepening gloom that settled upon the mind of Carlyle in his contempt of the humaner sentiment of his day, the way in which questions of practical philanthropy are dealt with by the school of Herbert Spencer, or what is said of the philosophy of Hartmann, as reflected in the dominant thought of Germany. Involuntarily, when we speak of " the fair humanities of old religion," we think not of the poetic paganism which Coleridge had in mind when he wrote the phrase, but of our own younger days, as compared with much of what we hear now. What attacks only the name and creed of Christianity may not alarm us much; but the spirit now described must give us pause, especially any symptoms of it which may have seized on the generation that is advancing to take our place.

But of this two things remain to be said.

The first is, that Science itself is really neutral, and not hostile. The representative minds of science are found on both sides of the line that marks the most radical difference of spiritual theory. And that, not only in the case of those who hold the two halves of their thought quite independent and distinct, — as it was said of Faraday, that when he went into his oratory he turned the key of his laboratory, — but with those like Carpenter, men of Christian habit and nurture, who with their best intelligence adjust and harmonize the two. We do not know what shape this adjustment may take in time to come; but we may be very sure that the higher nature of man will always claim its own right somehow.

> " That mind and soul according well
> May make one music, as before,
> But vaster " —

is the very meaning and motive of all sound religious thinking.

The other point is this: that, as Science affects to give no explanation or account of things, so these must always be suggested from another source. To say that we cannot discover or conceive the antecedents of the visible Universe is not to say that there are no such antecedents: it would weary us even to recount the postulates that must be assumed, to make the laws of heredity and natural selection intelligible or the process of them possible. To say that we can see nothing beyond the sensible horizon which bounds our life is not to say that there is nothing there: it is merely to leave the thought of the Unseen where it properly belongs, — to the heart or the imagination, as a celestial hope.

Physical science accounts for nothing. It must involve in its premises all it can possibly evolve in its results. Mere evolution from below — mechanical force working up into vital, mental, spiritual, without forethought or guidance anywhere — is as abhorrent to intellectual theory as it is to the moral sense, which postulates moral freedom. Somehow and somewhere — it would be truer to say, always and everywhere — Mind acts back on Things. The Cosmos itself is blank and unintelligible, except for some equivalent to the Christian faith in a Living God.

Turning now from the theoretical, let us consider next the practical side of the matter.

I do not think that, as a working faith, the religion of humanity is likely ever to show itself in a form more heroic, more devoted, more generous and tender, than what we have been familiar with under the older types of Christianity. From the very first,

the Christian faith has been a missionary faith. Its
message, with such understanding as men could have
of it, has been not to a select class or race, but to all
mankind. No "enthusiasm of humanity" is likely
hereafter to do more than rival the devotion of the
first martyr age, when the world lay under a horrible threefold yoke of superstition, corruption, and
despotism, and when the Christian salvation meant
deliverance from all three ; or the heroism of the
great missionary age, when the Church found such
servants as St. Martin, St. Severinus, St. Patrick, St.
Boniface, and St. Anschar to fight its battle with bar-
barism, and when its calendar was crowded with the
names of those who fought and fell in that greatest
warfare for humanity of all history; or the self-
sacrificing compassion of such more modern saints as
Francis Xavier and Charles Borromeo, who fulfilled
their mission of charity amid the miseries of famine
and pestilence that afflicted the sixteenth century;
or those missionaries of our day, who have carried
their message of divine compassion or their ready
hand to help, and have willingly laid down their
lives among the squalors of savagery, in the loneli-
ness of exile, in the reeking infection of plagues and
prisons and military hospitals,— from the resolute
and sober consecration of John Howard to those brave
women who have worn the red cross or the red cres-
cent through the horrors of the last Eastern war!

No form of piety or humanity in coming days is
likely to do more honor to the large sympathies of
which human nature is capable. It will be the
noblest of triumphs, if the world is able to keep

undiminished the splendid inheritance it has received in the record of these saintly Christian charities!

Why not, then, we may ask, simply keep that inheritance as we have received it, and so hand it down to posterity along with an improved theology?

That is just what we desire to do, but just where the difficulty lies. For the Christian charity of the past was not simply a sentiment; it was a conviction. It rested distinctly, though often unconsciously, on a notion of human nature and the Divine government, which necessarily passes away in the decay of the old theology.

That theology put vividly before the imagination these three things: first, the lost and miserable condition of mankind in its present state; second, the inexorable justice of God, along with his infinite but contingent mercy; third, the absolutely inestimable value of each single soul, in view of the eternity of glory or horror that certainly lay before it.

These three, intensely conceived as the most appalling, the most inspiring of realities, not only stirred every generous nature to rescue perishing men from their impending doom, but acted very powerfully on the springs of character and emotion in the soul itself, infinitely deepening and quickening the sentiment of compassion for human misery in every form. The brutal inhumanity of the ancients, the tender sentimentality so frequent in the modern world, hardly seem to belong to the same race of beings at anything like a similar stage of civilization. Part of the change is due to race, circumstance, mental refinement, or the mere softness of amiable ease; but a great part, and far the noblest part, in the modern sentiment of humanity is due to the eighteen centuries' assiduous culture of the Christian Church, resting distinctly on a theological basis, which as distinctly passes slowly and inevitably away.

Now while that sentiment in its integrity is the fairest and noblest thing our nature has to show, it becomes, when crippled and decayed, one of the most serious dangers, and offers one of the most serious difficulties, of the problem with which we have practically to do. Sentiment cut away from its intellectual base becomes sentimentalism. What was wholesome and strong becomes morbid and enfeebling. What was the soul of a vigorous body, once detached, remains a thin, restless ghost, a misleading phantom, a lying spirit. Thus love is better than faith or hope, says Paul; but not the "free love" of the modern evangel, — "free," because detached from faith or hope.

And so with the forms of active charity. If this life is necessarily a highway of misery and pain, leading to an eternity of bliss or woe, it is of small consequence that you show mere almsgiving to be a cause of more destitution than it heals. Whatever softens this rugged path to a single weary foot, even for a moment, is its own justification. Whatever multiplies, indirectly, the number of souls, candidates for eternal joys, and keeps them in that state of humiliation and dependence which is the best prelude to eternal joys, has in it the promise and the reward of ecclesiastical faith. But suppose the faith is gone, while the sentiment remains: then the same form of charity becomes half-hearted, weak, and mischievous. Suppose this life is *not* looked on as the inevitably painful and miserable highway to another. Suppose the faith in that other life to grow dim, and the fear of unending misery for a single human soul to be utterly passed away, — as the science and the compassionate temper of the modern world manifestly tend: what have we left but a sentimentalism, so to speak, without body and bones, — a direct hindrance instead of help to any wise, firm, lasting service we can hope to render to mankind?

The sentiment, then, assiduously nurtured for so many centuries by the Christian Church, gropes and pines for an intellectual foundation to take the place of that so deeply undermined. It is one of the dangers of a transition time like ours, that tenderness, sympathy, compassion, on the one side, and reason, intelligence, practical good sense, on the other, get alienated and divorced. The tender-hearted would inflict no pain; would take no man's life, even the guiltiest; would have all the suffering and dependent — the criminal, pauper, insane, idiotic, idle, or unemployed — share the comforts and luxuries which Nature makes the hard-earned reward of prudent toil. The cool reasoner sees that pain is often a part of the needful social surgery; that the choice must often be made between the life of the guilty and the safety of the innocent; that luxury and comfort, to those who have not earned or inherited them, mean a ruinous tax on industry and an enormous multiplication of the distresses it is sought to relieve.

Thus sentimentalism, from an inspiration of social

justice, becomes a disturbing element in social administration. Unless guided by a cool and even severe practical judgment, it serves directly to call out that cynic temper, bitterest enemy of humanity, which says: " Let the race, then, be to the swift, and the battle to the strong! Let the fittest survive as they may in the struggle of existence, where no quarter is given to the helpless and weak! Abolish all your charities: the experience of them only shows that they make more misery than they cure! Every man for himself, and the weakest to the wall!"

Now with Sentimentalism on one side and Cynicism on the other, there is only one possible way of reconciliation. It is *a theory of human life itself* sound enough to satisfy the reason, broad enough to admit all the sympathies and affections that brighten, comfort, purify, and bless. Such a theory men have found in the past, in an understanding of the Christian revelation which offered an object of our worship in a glorified Divine Humanity, and made the whole thought of this life solemn by the radiance or the shadow cast upon it from another sphere. And many of the best and bravest lovers of humanity in our day see no other solution to that grave question of the time than to go back, in humility and contrition, upon the path which the critical understanding has followed so far; to accept that yoke of doctrine and ordinance which, from being easy and light, had become too burdensome to be borne; and to restore — purified, no doubt, and enlightened — that spiritual supremacy which once made the Church the sovereign of all men's thoughts and lives.

This means, if we are consistent in our logic, to bring back, under modern conditions, the empire-church of the Middle Age. And I do not hesitate in the least to say, that, if our method in this thing is to be ecclesiastical at all, a Catholic Church such as we might easily conceive, under a spiritual head such as the present Pope appears to be, — grave, dignified, austere, cultivated, liberal of temper, — is by far the best and likeliest solution. It needs only a little of the wisdom of which that Church has shown itself capable in the past, to make it likely that very great multitudes of this and the coming generation will choose that way.

But I shall not speak here of the arguments for or against that consummation, or of anything that may be said of any form of compromise in the creeds of Protestantism. As I honestly think — though here I do not undertake to dogmatize — the ecclesiastical root out of which they all grow alike is withered, and will put forth no more new growth. At any rate, the order of thought with which we have most to do is absolutely detached from that root, and is growing in other soil. The intellectual foundation which we have to assume is laid not in Theology, but in Science. And, in dealing with any of the questions that touch the condition, the destinies, the religion of humanity, we must take in hand, first, the conceptions given us by Science. For the motive which Theology made strong and victorious in other days, we must substitute a motive, if we can, in keeping with the knowledge, thought, experience, and opinion of our own time.

I dislike to use in this connection the word "evolution," which has come to be a sort of catch-word, implying a dogmatism as sharp on one side as that it supplants on the other. But the accepted scientific theory of our time must at least contain the hint of the solution we seek. We shall find it (when we do find it at all), as that magnificent conception becomes familiar to us, suggested in the modern doctrine of evolution, — that our great, our real, religious task is *to aid in the unfolding of human nature, society, and life, toward the highest, noblest, fairest forms of which they are capable.* This, in its narrowest sense, is the "religion of humanity" as each one of us has to make it the personal task of his own life. This, in its broadest sense, is the "religion of humanity" as the object of scientific contemplation and an exalted speculative faith.

I do not go here into the details which a full illustration of this matter would demand. It is easy to see, however, that it contains the hint of what must serve to supply the place of the former dogmatism at almost every point. For example, the problem of Physical Evil: instead of making it the work of God's great Adversary ("an enemy hath done this"), modern thought makes it simply one phase of the inevitable "struggle for existence," which is the law of the animal creation; nay, wider, of the whole organio world. The problem of Moral Evil: instead of making it, as Milton does, "the ruin of our first parents," — a Fall, to be recovered by sacrifice and pain of expiation, — the modern view shows it to reside in that realm of passion and appetite which we share with all living creatures, by which they and we are equipped for that struggle of animal existence, — which is more and more put in the background and trampled under foot, in proportion as our human capacity and quality become developed. The theory of Moral Duty: it is made to depend no longer on the arbitrary edict of a Divine Sovereign, and the reward or penalty imposed by an Eternal Judge, but on those conditions of happiness and advancement, on the unfolding of the affections, sympathy, and sense of right, which are ascertained to be a part of the law of our being here.

I might continue this list through the whole catalogue of moral and religious obligations, or points of faith. But the obvious thing in them all is the very thing which I wish to emphasize. It is that, step by step, the theological is supplanted by the scientific, the divine by the human view. It is, in other words, a "religion of humanity," taking the place, in our generation, of a religion of theosophy. Its foundation is Law, not Dogma. Speculative theology has no longer any place in it, as defining arbitrarily the nature and character of our obligations, any more than it has in shaping our views of history and cosmogony.

The thought of a Divine existence, of an infinite Will, remains, — but only to give lift to imagination, gravity to reflection, reverence to the temper of the soul, and a foundation of gratitude and trust. Its value is less speculative than emotional. It is to be known not in dogmatic assertion, but through such symbol as we may imperfectly apprehend it by, —

the Life of the Universe, the Source of all Being, the Object of our adoration as we aspire more and more to the higher life. But when it comes to the task of interpretation and instruction and guidance, then it is the lesson of experience and the word of science that we need. History, politics, economy, social statics and dynamics, the laws of wealth, the laws of charity, the laws of character and heredity, the laws of population, the laws of crime, — these must make the subject-matter of our study, when we seek to follow out any line of practical duty and morals. It is with these, and not with any theological scheme of duty and opinion, that our nobler sentiments, our sweet and charitable emotions, will have to be reconciled.

One other step is needed, to give the full breadth of meaning in our phrase, "religion of humanity." It is very characteristic of the thought of the present day, that it has followed up, with extraordinary industry and zeal, the study of comparative religions. So long as Religion was thought of as consisting in one single, unalterable, revealed type of morals and doctrine, it had to be the religion of a race, creed, church, or dispensation, and not of humanity at large. As late as fifty years ago, to the average mind, the terms "Mahometan and Pagan" were enough to map out, rule out, cast contempt upon, all forms of faith outside the Christian world. Thus "Imposture" and "Idolatry" were the words sufficient to cover them all in a certain lofty, possibly pitying, condemnation: — at best pity; never an approach to sympathy or respect.

Contrast with this the wealth of knowledge, the greater accuracy of discrimination, the attitude even of discipleship toward special phases of mental or moral life, found in the study of the world-religions to-day! The patient, homely, plodding morals of Confucius; the charity, humility, and austerity of the Buddhists, with their strange tenderness to inferior creatures; the wild Brahman imagination, with its ancient and elevated forms of piety; the Parsee worship of Light and struggle with the powers of Darkness, from which the battle of Good and Evil was adopted into our own doctrinal tradition; the adventurous enthusiasm contrasting with the absolute submission of Islamism; "the fair humanities of old religion" in Greece and Rome, with what may be gathered from remoter Egypt and Assyria, — these make up the rich, varied, magnificently impressive panorama of the great faiths of mankind, before or beside the traditions of our Bible or creed. How striking, how immense the contrast presented in this view, when set beside the horror and repugnance of the early Church, and the virulent hate or else pitying scorn of the later Church, for all forms of faith except its own!

It is the task of the Religion of Humanity not simply to recognize the broad field of various beliefs in which the races of mankind have been trained, but, far more, to recognize whatever common spirit of justice, mercy, and truth may be in them all. It is not itself the creation of science, or the outgrowth of those comparative studies. It takes science for its instructor and guide; it takes comparative study for its wealth of illustration. But in itself it is that spirit of consecration to a better life, of willing service to mankind, which avails itself of these guides and helps. Its aim will be to gather and preserve whatever is good in the tradition to be found from every source. But for this it must have an independent life of its own, — as much as the corn that is planted or the acorn that is dropped in a soil enriched by the wash of a continent. Without it, the richest of soils will give us nothing but weeds. The characteristic life was hidden in the tree from which the acorn fell, or the harvest-field from which the corn was gathered.

It is the chief glory of Christianity to have secreted and ripened the seed that was to be cast into so generous a soil. The service of humanity hereafter may be more wise, more fruitful, more various; but it will never be more tender, generous, and devout than it has been during the long ages of its training. The dogmatic foundation it rested on so long is undermined and fast crumbling away. In that process of undermining, Unitarianism has had its share to do. A candid view of it will show that it has done its task, in the main, with a reverent, patient, honest, if not always a skilful hand. Partly in the work it has done, but much more in the minds it has nurtured and the souls it has comforted and fed, it has given its share towards preparing the way for a broader and stronger life.

VIII.

THE GOSPEL OF LIBERALISM.

MY object, in what I have now to say, will be to consider, as attentively as I can, some phases of religious thought and life which come nearest home to us, especially those included under the broad term Liberalism.

But I wish to hint, at the start, the limitation contained in the phrase "Gospel of Liberalism." A gospel is not a theory or a sentiment or a speculation or a creed. It is something greatly more noble and broad than either. It addresses not primarily the understanding or the affection, but the conscience and the soul. To the one, it is a law of life; to the other, it is a home of rest. It means an authority that commands obedience, and a deep foundation of spiritual peace. A gospel is something to live by, and it is also something to die by. Above is Duty, "stern daughter of the voice of God;" underneath are the Everlasting Arms. What we call a gospel, then, — as distinct from a theory, a sentiment, a speculation, or a creed, — contains these two fundamental elements of the religious life. And it is in view of these — that is, with a practical and not a speculative aim — that I shall attempt to trace some of the bearings of our position, here and now.

For the Harvard Divinity School has been connected, in a very special way, with the history of religious liberalism in this country, and is responsible for a good many of its features. I need not recite the list of bright names that are scattered along its record, running back now sixty-five years, — that is, nearly two generations of the sons of men. You will recall them easily in one swift glance of memory; and you will see how they not only include those names of love and honor which represent the modester learning and soberer piety of an earlier time, but cover the most radical and brilliant thought of a younger generation, that are rapidly pushing us who stand on the ripe side of fifty towards the eternal shadow. It is not for us, certainly not to-day, so much as by a thought or hint, to disown either portion of a life so broad and ample. If I might be allowed to say a word for myself, it would be that my heart lives so largely in the gracious and venerable past of our communion, and that my thought goes forward with so keen and active sympathy with those younger minds to whom the privilege of my place brings me into daily near relation, that it would be impossible for me to say a word that should put me, consciously, at difference with a single phase of it that has been honestly thought or lived.

And yet my purpose is as far as possible from the vague glorying and complacency which are often in what we say when we speak of the triumphs and advances of liberal thought. On the contrary, the temper in which we have just now to regard the situation is that which sees it as grave, perhaps critical; at least, which is willing to see what there is in it of grave and critical. Of all forms of Epicurean delight, perhaps the most repugnant to such a temper is the easy-going optimism which turns religion into an idle sentiment, and parades, under the name "liberal," an inane triumph at the mere levelling of the shrines of an austerer faith. The walls of old Error may fall to the sound of trumpets and shouting. The bulwarks and palaces of the new City of God will never be built but through skill and patience and toil and prayer and pain, one hand holding a weapon to strike for the Truth, the other a tool to build for the Life.

I do not speak of our denominational fortunes, or the prospects of any particular form of opinion and belief that we may hold in common. But it is true, now as ever, that the Power which presides in human things exacts heavy pledges of fidelity of the agents honored and commissioned to do its work. The prophetic office was evermore a "burden;" and it was never taken up with a light heart by any one worthy and fit to carry it. He is "driven of the Spirit," like Jesus. A "necessity is laid upon him," like Paul. And, as Milton says, "When God commands to take the trumpet, and blow a dolorous or jarring blast, it lies not in man's will what he shall say or what he shall conceal." The occasion is always great to him who can conceive it greatly. And the greatness of the occasion is measured not by the joy and applause alone, or the expanding sense of power, but by the pain and fear and danger of the way, and by the weight of that burden of misery and want and crime which our Gospel is commissioned to relieve.

So, then, what we mean by a "Gospel of Liberalism," if there is such a thing, is not a theory that fits smooth and soft to the methods of our understanding; not a sentiment, bright, comfortable, and sweet to the moods of our emotion. Nor is it even, in a more generous way, that large sympathy and satisfaction with which we feel ourselves to walk in the direction of the world's progress, and to work in the front lines of the world's work.

It is not summed up, again, in the word Culture, which had a certain claim to be the gospel of half a century ago, — no matter how large, rich, and deep the sense we give that word; any more than in the older and profounder word Salvation, narrowed to mean our own rescue from the wrath to come. Its watchword is at once lowlier and nobler, — that is, Service. And it is not till we have measured the whole sweep of the peril, the terror, and the wrong from which mankind is to be delivered; not till we have sounded that deep sea of unbelief, ungodliness, despair of the future, which threatens to drown men, as of old, in destruction and perdition; not till we know in our hearts the hollowness of a refined materialism and the empty mockery of its Epicurean creed, — that we begin to know the privilege and the burden that belong to our better faith.

Now I have been using words and phrases and availing myself of sentiments which belong, as some would say, to the old theology, and have no place left in the smooth and comfortable Liberalism of the day.

The Devil is dead, they say, and the fires of hell are put out. What need have we of salvation, and what meaning can we find in it? If any should say this, or feel this, then I should reply that that is just the fallacy it is our business to meet. We have a message to the world of some sort; at least, we think we have, or else it is with very vain thoughts indeed that we undertake to meet the life-problems which occupy us to-day. The adequacy of that message depends on our being able to share not only the fresh vigor and breadth of modern thought, but the sweetness, the fervor, the devout aspiration, the hate of evil also, and the consecrated will, which are the sacred traditions and the birthright of our Christian faith.

In what is left for me to say, I shall attempt, if not to interpret that message, at least the more modest task of grouping a few points that may help show the direction in which the interpretation is to be found. It is properly of two sorts, — theoretic or intellectual, and religious or practical. A few words are due to each.

Of the first, I will only say that for the intellectual solution of the questions which lie so near our thought, — what is sometimes called the reconciliation of knowledge and faith, — I am sure that we must look a great way farther off than most of us have been accustomed to think. By this I mean a solution accepted by the thinking world at large: we all, I trust, have found the practical solution to the problem of our own life. But, more broadly, we have thus far only secured (more or less completely) the mutual independence of Science and Religion.

For their mutual harmony we have doubtless very long to wait. It is told of the statesman Cavour, that, not long before his death, he said those of the younger generation were to be envied; for, before the end of the century, they would witness the grandest of historical events, the birth of a new religion. Prophets, says Mr. Martineau, are apt to be mistaken in their dates. I suppose that what Cavour had in mind was some Positivist conception, more or less distinctly realized, of what is coming to be called "the religion of humanity." Whether that or not, at all events he meant some sort of "consensus" or reconciliation — some visible organization, perhaps — of sentiment, thought, and life, which are so grievously at discord now.

But any "positive" theory of knowledge is very far, as yet, from making the basis of a religion. For the realization he talked of it would be cheap to wait not twenty years, but ten or twenty times as long. Consider that it has already taken four hundred years, since the ghastly collapse of Mediæval faith, to bring us where we are. Consider the tasks of scientific theology yet before us, hardly attempted or begun; consider the slow development of an independent ethics, large and delicate enough to take in all the complexities of modern life: — and these are but two of the conditions. Any perspective shallower than that of centuries will scarce give us the equipoise we need, in dealing with so large issues.

We are working unconsciously — we ought to be working consciously — for a future that is a great way off. The intellectual patience so essential, without any lack of ethical fervor, can absolutely be had only by the familiar habit of dealing with historic periods and long lapses of time. "Providence," says some French writer, "moves through time as the gods of Homer through space : it takes a step, and ages have rolled away." But we fidget and are impatient. At every little advance of our knowledge we must out with our pocket-rule, and measure how the new piece will fit the majestic heavens and the rolling earth. At each fresh phrase of each new school in meta-physics we fancy we have found, at length, an ade-quate theory of creation and providence. These theories, all the way from Plato down to Spencer, are the playthings of the mind ; and we use them, as children do, in childlike unconsciousness of the dif-ference in scale between those crystal spheres and our round nursery globes. In my own brief recollection, two or three very promising theories of the universe have come up as a flower and been cut down ; and I fully expect to outlive that which seems most fash-ionable now.

I have no mind here to criticise the philosophy of Evolution, so called, either for attack or defence. That task should be left to competent specialists. An amateur in such things is apt to be a bungler, and most of us are amateurs. It would even be an impertinence in me to say that I accept the theory, — except as probably the most instructive, certainly the most entertaining, way to co-ordinate and har-monize certain known facts, and help us deal with them practically ; not at all to account for them, in any philosophical sense, theoretically. To account for facts of life by laws of growth, for existence by laws of similitude and succession of phenomena, is too plain a solecism to need more than an allusion to it here. It is only the presumption which some expounders of the new creed have found in it, in the direction of fatalism and denial of the moral life, that justifies even this allusion.

Not that these premature assumptions are matter of complaint or regret from our point of view. On the contrary, it is ground of real congratulation, as regards the true interests of the religious life, that the theory has been run out so fast in the direction of blank and blind Necessity; that Fatalism has shown its hand, before the capacity of devout emotion or moral enthusiasm had been slowly smothered under it. The brutal materialism which we have seen cited in Büchner's exposition of it strikes quick, like those swift sounding-leads that go like a bullet into the sea-depths, against the indomitable bottom fact of human consciousness, the sense of moral freedom. As soon as we see just what that logic can do, and just how far it will go, we may breathe free again, and take up, cheerily and patiently as before, the suspended thread of the *religious* evolution.

Our relation as "scientific" theologians to the larger world of science is at once that of willing learners, and of independent co-workers and explorers. We want the enterprise and courage of natural science, not its limitations; its freedom, not its bondage or constraint; most of all, its affirmations; least of all, its denials. What it can give us we take for our help; but there is no need that we put ourselves in servitude to any man or creed or school that claims to speak its final word. We have to do, not with cosmogonies, whether gnostic or agnostic, or with theories about the origin of the lower forms of life. Our proper business is with the highest forms of all. We were not in at the birth of things, and we shall not be in at the death. Not where life begins, and not where it ends, but where it culminates, is the portion of it given us to explore.

Our business, as explorers, is with primary facts of human experience, and with what, in scientific phrase, are called " laws of similitude and succession" of those facts; that is, the laws of human character, human life, human destiny, within the horizon that bounds our observation. The "phenomena" we have to watch include the height of aspiration, the depth of passion and contrition, the wealth of experience, which make up the higher life of men. The "facts" we are called to study and account for are known by such grand names as salvation, regeneration, atonement, holiness, religious peace, faith, self-knowledge and self-conse-cration born out of conviction and experience of sin. These, on their human side at least, are neither "unprovable" nor "unverifiable."

Now those great words mean something: for us, not (it may be) dogmatically, but at any rate relig-iously. It is our business to find out what they mean. Their religious sense, rightly caught, becomes their scientific sense. Most likely we reject the dog-matic sense fastened on them in the old theology. But the moment we ask what brought them into use at all, what has given them their weight and power as factors in human life, we see that we are dealing with the very foundation-stones of character and conduct. While Christianity is the accepted interpreter of those words, so long she holds the key of the moral situation. Without that key, " Science, falsely so called," can only grope and fumble about the lock.

No theory of life that ever was invented — of its transmission or development — claims any respect from us as religious thinkers, that does not take in the full meaning of those words, as standing for phases of human consciousness and for great facts of human history. If there is such a thing as a "scientific theology," its function is to be found, not in slavishly adopting the dicta or the deductions that have been found valid in the lower ranges of being, but in adding our independent share, as students and explorers, to that common stock of data and postulates, from which any theory of life worth having must be deduced.

Our especial field is those moral forces which lie back of men's character and conduct; or, on a larger scale, those strong tides of passion which have borne forward the great procession of human institutions and events. We are not going to accept that cheap and easy theory about these things, which simplifies the problem by ignoring the most complex and important of its conditions. The highest fact in human nature is as much a fact, and as valid in its way, as any number or any co-ordination of lower facts. Whatever view we choose to take of the Universe at large, a soul is at least as near the origin of life as a mollusk or a stone. Into whatever forms of fact we translate our thought, the thought remains true that Life ebbs and flows in the veins of the mighty Mother that has borne us all, and has its source in the Heart of all things, which we can call only mysterious and Divine.

And now, a word as to the situation. A few years ago grave warning was given, under the alarm-cry "Rocks Ahead," of a widening gulf between the popular faith and the belief or no-belief of educated minds. Our own public has heard something since of the peril of a "moral interregnum," and of "certain dangerous tendencies in American life," threatening from the divorce which to many eyes seems imminent between the science and the religion of our time. I take these hints simply to fix our point of view, not seeking to add emphasis to them by any words of mine. After all, the spectre of doubt or disbelief must be looked straight in the face, to see what it really is. It will not vanish by any pious closing of our eyes to it.

The problem, to be sure, is no new one. It is just over seven hundred years since the Mediæval Church, startled from its sense of secure dominion, began to feel its way slowly, with many a misgiving and horrible recoil, towards the suppression of dissent by force. What that led to, we know by such names of terror and hate as the Inquisition and the Wars of Religion. Those methods are now by some three centuries happily obsolete. What we have now to heed is not so much the world's hate as its indifference and contempt, — a phenomenon new to our time, in strong contrast to the passions and violences of the past. A thousand years ago the social force, the active thought, the political life, drifted just as steadily towards the great Catholic organization as they are drifting from it now. Alliance of Church and Empire was as natural, as needful then as the divorce of secular and spiritual authority is seen to be to-day. Charlemagne was as much a product of his time as Gladstone and Bismarck are of ours.

Let us reflect a moment on the significance and the bearing of that change. Its movement is like that of the Drift Period in geology. Its ultimate sources are in the elemental life of things ; its sweep lies far beyond the strength of the strongest will, the craft of the most skilful policy, to control. That is why we call it "drift": its course is determined not by conscious engineering, but by granite walls of circumstance. Hildebrand and Barbarossa break vainly, alike, against those adamant bounds. Their work is caught up and swept on, alike, by that resistless flood. At best, we may do something to understand the course and sweep of great historic forces. It is not likely that any effort or thought of ours will do much to help or thwart them.

But, indirectly, thought may do something to control the movement which it is impotent of itself to create or check. Else, why endure the burden and pain that go with all serious thinking ? Even that vast curve, which at first sight seems to trace out fatally the orbit of human things, it may be possible to deflect a little, as soon as we can read its formula and understand the law of its generation. Events in the large are ordered by a Power as much beyond our comprehension as beyond our reach. Events in detail are ruled for the time by passion, compulsion, and authority. Providence is on the side of the strongest regiments, when a particular issue is to be fought out. But in the long run of any one generation, — much more, of a hundred years, or of twenty generations, — the course of events is guided by the course of general opinion. Thought is the engineer that traces the channel of the stream, deepening it here, cutting it off there, and so at length controlling its direction. Science finds and equips the pioneers, who go in advance of those strongest regiments. Its pioneer work, for us, has been well and thoroughly done. Liberalism, following close, is already well able to hold the field of mind. There is little to dread from the spiritual despotisms of the past. Whatever disturbance religious passion may bring into the political conflicts of the day, Thought at least is free. , A reaction towards ecclesiastical tyranny is neither possible (we may hope), nor even conceivable.

Yet Liberalism cannot afford to extenuate or disparage the forces of its two great adversaries, Ecclesiasticism and Dogma. Outside the range of pure intellect, it is as yet far inferior to either. In the sphere of religious education, pious emotion, and moral influence, the Papal Church is all the stronger, perhaps, since twelve years ago it was disencumbered of its hampering temporalities. One word from the Vatican to-day could stir or still a tempest of religious fanaticism in Dublin, Vienna, or Warsaw; in Quebec, New

York, or San Francisco. Rome has even some special advantage here, in the easiness of our laws, in the enormous accumulation of untaxed property, and especially in the great immigration of its obedient subjects, who vote as they are told, whose party leaders are true to that one interest, and who have been said to hold twice as much political power as so many Protestants, owing to their remarkable skill in multiplying votes. It is not for us in America, at least, to think lightly of that power.

So too, religiously, Liberalism is far inferior to that pliant, zealous, many-headed, many-handed organization known as Protestantism, even to the feeblest of its congeries of sects and creeds. Broken and weak as it may seem, looked at intellectually, Protestantism is yet, looked at religiously, the chief single force in the three great political systems of England, Germany, and America. It has command of prodigious wealth, and includes a large part of the wealth-producing skill of the world. It has still a very large and enthusiastic body of adherents, whose zeal it keeps up by great generous enterprises, such as missions, charities, and education. It has immense resources at its command, to nurture the religious sentiment, to cultivate religious sympathies, and to inculcate religious belief. Not, certainly, with a futile and vain notion of its weakness, but with a distinct apprehension of its very great and still preponderating strength, should we suffer ourselves to speak of its system of opinion (which we are so apt to do) as doomed and perishing. It may be so; but not yet, not in our day.

Of Protestantism as dogma we take the less account, however, since in the argument it rests on is the one fatal weakness: it must appeal to Reason to maintain itself against a claim of authority far weightier and older; it must appeal to its own slender Authority to defend itself against the reason it has invoked. Protestantism as a life has been very great and noble. As dogma, it has been simply an expounding and attenuating of the older creed. For theology, it still remands us to Augustine, Aquinas, or the Reformers of the sixteenth century. It has gained little in these three hundred years, except the accumulation of great stores of learning, most of it valuable only as material for the historian or antiquary; while in the same period it has lost its militant, heroic, aggressive character, and been put at heavy disadvantage in the fight. It is never once thought of by sagacious Catholics as a formidable, hardly even as a serious, enemy. The political power of Protestant countries they may very likely fear and hate; but Protestantism as a system of thought serves them only (so to speak) as a break-water, protecting them, so far as it goes, from the only enemy they do fear, — namely, Modern Science, and the unbelief that comes from science, against which, with pathetic simplicity, the present Pope is setting up the interior pasteboard defences of Scholasticism.

Sentimentally, Protestantism helps to keep up the tradition of ecclesiastical authority, in belief and practice, with the unwholesome craving for it; and so plays fatally into the hands of its opponent. Intellectually, Catholic theologians hold their Protestant adversaries (justly or not) simply in contempt, or at least take pains to make us think so. Their own learnin is at least equal; their reliance on authority is far more consistent and distinct. But behind Protestantism itself there is a spirit and a power disowned of Protestantism, which they do fear, — a spirit and a power which they know they will have to meet presently, and take account with, face to face. They understand, as well as we, that the really formidable alternative is not "Protestant or Catholic," but " Reason or Rome."

There would be something ludicrous in the large and confident way we sometimes have in speaking of these things, if we only said them as Unitarians; that is, as the smallest of Protestant sects, disowned or ignored by nearly all the rest. Why we speak largely and confidently is because we feel ourselves consciously allied with vaster forces, which we are assured will have the heritage of the future. Personally, I am a Unitarian, and hold that birthright very dear; just as historically I am a Christian, ecclesiastically a Protestant, and hold that birthright very dear. But, as students of opinions and forces, we are obliged to take in a much larger field. It is on that large field that we must watch the slow unfolding of human thought. We cannot go back on the pathway which the human mind has followed in its irresistible advance. We cannot unsay the word, or undo the work, which has reduced not only these beliefs and dogmas of the past, but the forms of experience they grew from, within the categories and methods of scientific criticism. From that tribunal it is too late in the day to hold any mode of opinion, or any moment of evolution, secluded and enshrined. Our view of the Past must be swift enough and broad enough at least to guess what the coming stage of development is to be.

A single aspect of this wide view is all that concerns us now. Let us look a moment, then, at the supplanting of the received Cosmologies by larger and more precise conceptions of Nature and Life, with the resulting effect on current religious ideas.

Five hundred years ago, Dante's scheme — of Hell as a great cavern running through the earth, of Purgatory as a hill on the other side, and of Paradise as filling the nine concentric celestial spheres — was a fair enough picture of the way the most highly educated looked on things ; a long advance on the earlier notion of the earth as a four-square plane, patterned like the tabernacle of Scripture, with the lake of fire below, and the solid crystal vault above. Copernicus was ten years older than Martin Luther ; and his system (which Melanchthon would have violently suppressed, as atheism) gave the first, by far the rudest, shock the old belief has ever felt.

Think of the steps that have been taken since : — Galileo's discoveries about the planets, suggesting a plurality of inhabited worlds ; Kepler's laws of planetary motion, dissolving away the solid spheres of the old astronomy ; Newton's theory of universal gravitation, displacing arbitrary will as the direct cause of the celestial motions ; Franklin's proof that lightning and electricity are the same, doing away the superstitious awe at thunder-storms ; Laplace's nebular hypothesis, so generally accepted, carrying back the origin of the solar system to incalculable remoteness; Dalton's demonstration of definite proportions and elective affinities in chemistry, making ridiculous the old notion of "dead matter" as the antithesis of Spirit or the enemy of Good; demonstration of the speed of light and distances of the stars, destroying utterly the old belief in a local heaven; geological proofs of the uniformity of cosmic forces and antiquity of the globe, disproving absolutely the popular chronology of creation; discoveries of the spectroscope as to the atmosphere of the sun and the light of stars, widening enormously and at once the range of our physics; the well-established doctrine of the conservation and equivalence of energy, with its far-reaching effect on our conception of the laws of life; and now the scheme of evolution by natural process, apparently destined, with whatever modification, to supersede and swallow up every other theory of the trans- mission of life and the inheritance of natural good or evil.

These successive steps — near half of them taken within living memory — interest us chiefly, not as so many advances or conquests of human intellect, but as they bear on conceptions and ideas which were once wrought up without question into men's relig- ious belief, and were held necessary to their salvation. It is very impressive to survey those steps in their connection and in their order of sequence, if we only stop a moment to reflect how prodigious is the men- tal revolution they imply. To take one step the other way, to roll back by ever so little an arc the driving-wheel of that revolution, is manifestly impossible. And the steps have been coming with increasing frequency and increasing weight.

With a wise instinct, the Church — or the theological spirit it had trained — tried to throttle at the birth those twin earth-born giants, Natural Science and Free Thought. It burned Giordano Bruno. It silenced Galileo in the cells of its Inquisition. It allowed the Newtonian theory to be taught only when it became absolutely necessary in courses of the higher mathematics, and then only as hypothesis, never as fact. It continued to pray for rain and against thunder, and so continues to this day. It protected the first chapter of Genesis by frivolous and grotesque interpretations, and tries so to protect it now. It insisted that fossil remains were manufactured in that shape by the Almighty, and packed into rock-strata when the earth was built. And its advance lines are only beginning to fall back from the defences, somewhat hastily thrown up, to resist the threatened attack of the new philosophy of Evolution.

The tendency which these things indicate, it is safest for us to accept as fixed and inevitable. It is no part of our business to add to their momentum, or to oppose any feeble check of our own. We may as well think of trying to push on the rapids above Niagara ; we may as well think of trying to stop them. Our only concern with them, as religious thinkers, is to see, as clearly as we can, how they touch or define for us the conditions of religious thought.

But observe, again, that all this series of great

shocks against the ancient faith have affected only what was outside and incidental. They have not touched what is inward and essential. Religion may yet be saved whole and unharmed, we think; but only by that cordial co-working with the spirit of the time, which is the very thing we mean by a *liberal* faith. And what does this imply?

Liberalism is not a code of opinion. It is simply a habit of mind, making the atmosphere of one's opinions. What those opinions are depends on a great many things. Sometimes they will be such as to keep one very close to the old theology and the believers in it; only, while theirs is a dogmatic, his is a sentimental belief. Sometimes they will be such as to repel him violently from them, and put him in the attitude of aggressive radicalism. But, in general, it is away from, not towards, the established creed. It begins, for example, with criticism of text or doctrine; it goes on with more and more searching criticism of the Sacred Books themselves; until it sets seriously about the task (which is that of the more advanced scholarship now) of bringing the entire record under the generally received canons that apply to all histories of men and all growths of opinion.

Of course, it tends thus to discard miracle in the sacred narrative: not that it necessarily denies the facts which looked miraculous once, but that, when it accepts them (as Dr. Furness does), it seeks to put a natural interpretation on them; and this, while it leaves unimpaired their value as appeals to pious sentiment, quite destroys their value as evidences of religious dogma.

It rejects, without hesitation or fear, all doctrines —such as election, reprobation, and an endless hell— which affront either reason or natural justice or the character of the Divine government. It loves to recognize what is attractive in other forms of religion, —as Buddhism, Brahmanism, and the rest,—sometimes to the unjust disparagement of Christianity. It inclines strongly to humanity, kindliness, natural charity, as against set acts of piety, in its view of human duty. In its social theory, it disinclines just as strongly to admit the hard facts or accept the hard conditions of human life. Its working plans are at once expanded by a generous sympathy, and weakened by an amiable sentimentalism. Its moral peril is, of too strong recoil from austere bigotry to indolent laxity of judgment. And it too easily admits an over-conceit of itself, which leads to spiritual impoteney, cowardice, and self-indulgence.

Away from this moral peril, the great glory and strength of Liberalism are in its cheerful, courageous, confident piety. The sweetest of hymns and the serenest of good lives have flowed from it. Passion and fervor of the religious life it is apt to lack. That spirit belongs rather to a more stern and ascetic faith. It comes from a sense of terror, a depth of contrition, a gratitude for rescue, which Liberalism cannot feel, since the only God it knows is a God of love. And it is weak in this, that it does not recognize — what Nature alike and the deep conviction of sin declare — a God of terror and a God of wrath, as well.

In the several forms in which we have known it hitherto, Liberalism has given to the world many of the noblest, purest, gently serene, obedient, and holy lives. But of itself, and intellectually regarded, it is only a step of transition. It is very far, in any exposition it has made of itself as yet, from even attempting to state a theory of the Divine government so as to take in the dark side of it, as Calvinism did. It is very far now from being a great power to move the world, as Calvinism was. It is, as we may say, the religious, pietistic, sentimental side of our modern thought. It serves, at best, but as a set-off to the harder and more practical, the positive, the scientific side. And our best wish for it is that it may survive as the gracious, beaming, benignant soul, making glad, hopeful, and bright a world whose glory seemed threatening to depart.

For, as we cannot fail to see, those steps of mental revolution which I have spoken of have seemed to many grave thinkers the coming on of the chill penumbra that betokens before long a total eclipse of faith. Even if it were so, the body that intercepts the light is, after all, a celestial body, though earthy and opaque, and its shadow will doubtless presently pass away.

And there is compensation, even here. We may, indeed, for a generation or two, lose that near and comforting assurance of the Divine Personality which, I am sure, will come back to us in a glorified form when our minds are grown to apprehend the conditions under which it must be held. As it has been held by many, and still is, it is a mere idolatry — sometimes cringing and cowardly, sometimes insolently familiar — which we shrink from as blasphemy, often, in the prayers we hear and the threats addressed to men's religious terror. If our speculations on the Divine Nature fail us, let us first think worthily of the divine reality in life. Then, it may be, we shall have clearer vision of the Living God, who is the fountain of universal life.

So, too, it may be needful that men should lose for a season their clear and vivid conviction of the Future Life, — seeing what evil use has been made of it in the craven fears and selfish hopes that have constituted the buttress of ecclesiastical tyranny; seeing how multitudes of religionists have deliberately sacrificed the urgent duties and forgotten the deep wrongs and griefs of the life that now is, in their self-indulgent brooding on joys or terrors of the life to come. It were better for us all to ask less how we may be *sure* than how we may be *worthy* of that incomprehensible and august destiny. The nobility of the Hebrew race began when it left behind the Egyptian creed of another life, and entered on the wilderness of wandering and pain, believing only in the present Deity; when it cast aside the "Book of the Dead," with all that solemn ritual and imagery, and the grave judgments of Osiris beyond the dark river, and accepted instead, for its sole portion, the Ten Commandments, as it began its bleak but valiant march. From that seed grew its later, better faith in immortality, and the larger life which is ripening to-day.

If it is true, then, — and I do not say that it is, though many will say it for me, — that there is going to be an eclipse, for longer or shorter, of those two great lights of faith, one of two things will certainly occur. Either our intellectual creed will drift steadily into that sombre pessimism which is the last word of a merely fatalistic evolution, while a practical materialism will come more and more to hold the field, in a godless science, a ruder scramble for wealth, a baser giving up of ourselves to sensual delight, a widening of the insolent and cruel distinctions of rich and poor, learned and ignorant, with the ever-impending danger of a war of classes, threatening to blot out the glory and life of civilization itself, — that on the one hand; or, on the other hand, salvation must be found where it has been ever of old, in deepening and renewing the springs of life in the soul itself.

And here we must bear in mind that, while nothing we can do or say or think can alter in the least the FACT of the Divine government or our own ultimate destiny, yet our own relation to that government or that destiny depends wholly on what we do and think and are. The lessons of Christian history, which make by far the most profound and instructive chapter in the moral history of mankind, have taught us little, unless they have shown how salvation, at the hour of extreme crisis, has always been found in one way, — that is, *by returning upon the deepest moral convictions of the soul.*

Not speculation, not emotion, but Conscience is the true foundation of the higher life. It has always begun with an intense conviction of Sin and sense of personal need, or else with an intense perception of the Evil in the world to be overcome by good. It has always worked out in a new freshness and vigor in the sense of right and wrong, in a more living conception of practical righteousness. It was so with Jesus; it was so with Paul; it was so with Augustine; it was so with Luther; it was so with those disciples who one by one embraced the stern, sad, valiant creed of Calvin, and through it saved to the modern world most of what makes its life worth saving. With each of them, it was associated with doctrines, or forms of thought, which are seen now to be outgrown, and which the world must soon inevitably leave behind, — with false Messianic hopes; with crude anthropologies; with dogmatic creeds, strange and effete; with impossible socialistic dreams. But with each of them it has left not only great examples of personal fidelity: it has left also a distinct lesson, as needful to-day as then. It is a very pitiful and meagre thing to have exposed their error, unless we have grasped and interpreted their truth.

And, finally, what is that truth, as it bears now on our thought and life?

For answer, think what it was at the time of the decline and fall of Rome. Then, as now, there was a system of material fatalism [1] coming to be widely accepted among cultivated minds. Then, as now, old creeds were dissolving. The restraints of ancient piety being loosed, whole communities were plunged into scepticism, and with that into the luxuries and vices for which scepticism offers a cheap and easy excuse to self-indulgence. Imperial Rome was then what, with a startling likeness, imperial Paris seemed

[1] Under the name Manichæan, — see "Fragments," etc., pp. 131–133.

fifteen years a o. And then the key to a nobler life for Humanity was found in the soul of one man,[1] who with passionate earnestness sought to cleanse himself of his personal share of guilt, and so found anew the sense of moral freedom, and the solution of his life's problem, in absolute surrender of himself to an Almighty Will.

Now, whatever else the course of thought may leave behind, it remains that every man of healthy intelligence knows there is a Right and there is a Wrong, and that the difference between them measures the highest law of his being. The foundations of the Universe are far, very far, beyond our sight; but we know they must be laid in equity. There is "an Eternal, not ourselves, that makes for righteousness."

> " If this fail,
> The pillared firmament is rottenness,
> And earth's base built on stubble."

This deepest law of our life we cannot always learn by way of theory. So much of it as concerns ourselves we learn by way of obedience. One may be our Theology; the other is our Religion. When the desire to know and the purpose to obey have taken full possession of a man ; when they mount in his aspiration, and flame in his passion, and breathe in his piety, and give their color to his thought, and nerve him to his work, — then we have the true Religion which our time demands, independent of all its Philosophies, and nobler than all its Creeds.

[1] Saint Augustine.

APPENDIX.

MEMORIAL ADDRESS

Spoken on the 30th of May, 1882 (Decoration Day), at the Annual Meeting of the American Unitarian Association.

BY REV. FREDERIC H. HEDGE, D.D.

MR. PRESIDENT, — We do well to devote a portion of this anniversary day of our Association to the memory of those servants of our cause who during the past year, having finished their work, have retired from our ranks to "join the choir invisible."

HENRY W. BELLOWS.

It falls to me to speak of Dr. Bellows, who, if less impressive as a preacher than the honey-lipped Nestor[1] who hastened to follow him in death, has had in all our annals no equal as a man of action.

Two years ago, we celebrated the memory of that illustrious divine[2] whom we regard as our father in the faith. To-day, we commemorate the disciple and brother by whose organizing genius that faith has been made to take to itself a body as compact as our unformulized theology and the right to differ, which we all claim, will allow.

[1] Dr. Dewey.   [2] Dr. Channing.

He was our Bishop, our Metropolitan. The dignity is unknown by name in our communion: the office has no place in our acephalous, isocratic polity. But this once in our history, by this one man in our brotherhood, the function was exercised, and that by no robbery but by universal consent of the brethren. It was no rape of clerical ambition, but a lot which fell to him by native gift. He took possession of his see by supreme right of natural leadership and self-evident vocation, — a see extending from the Bay of Fundy to the Golden Gate. An ecclesiastical Centurion, "set under authority," he said to this man, "Go," and he went; to another, "Come," and he came. He ordered us hither and thither, and we surrendered ourselves to his ordering. One day, he summoned us to New York, and founded the National Conference of Unitarian Churches. Another day, he summoned us to Springfield, and established the Ministers' Institute. These organizations, which we trust will survive him and last as long as our communion shall maintain its specialty and continue a separate fold in universal Christendom, testify of his far-seeing sagacity as well as his far-reaching zeal. They are his monument, had he no other. They are his "epistle written in our hearts, known and read of all men," — "written not with ink, but with the spirit of the living God."

St. Paul, enumerating the trials and triumphs of his mission, boasts that he was "in journeyings often." Our Unitarian missionary, in journeys not less frequent, exceeded, if journeys be estimated according to their length, by many a meridian the apostolic mark. When Starr King died, he hastened to San Francisco, while as yet no rail had pierced the Rocky Mountains, comforted the orphaned diocese, with counsel and ordinance confirmed the church, and established a pastor in the vacant pulpit. This was one among many of the generous impromptus of his alert and enterprising spirit.

His qualifications for the office he assumed were, first of all, faith in the cause and fervent love of the cause he espoused. With the heart, and not with the understanding only, he believed in the liberal gospel of our Church. With the heart he desired to see it prevail and extend its beneficent influence in the land. He was not content to hold the beliefs he cherished as a private estate. The doctrine by which he had been enlightened and cheered and inspired he burned to impart to others for their enlightenment, encouragement, and inspiration. He believed in its final triumph, but not without adequate efforts devoted to that end. Those efforts, so far as he was concerned, should not be wanting.

To these moral incentives we must add a felicitous tact and extraordinary power of adaptation. He discerned two hostile forces at work : on the one hand, a headlong, radical spirit tending to Nihilism ; on the other, a timid, conservative temper threatening arrest in the past and captivity to dogma and the letter. He set himself to mediate between the two. His own theological proclivities inclined to the conservative side, but his convictions were not very exigent. He could practise a tolerant frankness, which by conciliating dissent might limit the aphelion of denial, while it shamed stagnation and loosened the bands of custom.

He craved popularity, he needed it for the end he had at heart. And he *was* popular. Innocent of duplicity, by virtue of a never-failing suavity, he could be all things to all men, conciliating the self-willed, humoring the weak, noticing the obscure, acknowledging the claims of the eminent, paying tribute where it was due, and collecting it from all. Always the man he talked with deemed him his particular friend. There was no falsity in this and no hypocrisy : it was pure affability, the easy libation of a fluent nature and a brimming cup.

I note in this man the rare combination of the consecrated soul with the boon companion, the enthusiast with the man of the world. He was not one of those of whom it could be said, as Wordsworth said of Milton, "His soul was as a star, and dwelt apart." He was not one of the bloodless hermit saints, who seem not to belong to this world, attached to it by only the slenderest thread of animality, whose soul

> "Scarce touching where it lies,
> But gazing back upon the skies,
> Shines with a mournful light."

He was no ghost, no lank ascetic, but an honest, wholesome son of earth, at home in the flesh, who without being in the least a sensualist, not living by bread *alone*, yet lived by bread in the widest sense, — a boon companion who enjoyed the feast and the jest, could give as well as take of that coin, was quick at repartee, met the worldling on his own ground, and charmed the table with the brightness of his wit. Yet he never unfrocked himself, nor pained his friends with any sense of incongruity between his discourse and his calling. As in Philip Neri, the jester was the foil of the priest.

Withal, as I said, a consecrated soul. If he shone as a man of the world in worldly converse, he had none the less his conversation in heaven. His supreme aim in life, embracing and subordinating all secondary aims, was in one or another way, by this or that ministry, to fix and extend the kingdom of heaven on the earth, everywhere rooting out evil and planting good. For this and in this he lived and moved and had his being. Time, money, and pen were at the service of every good cause. In what charity was he not active? In what philanthropic movement did he not lead? As champion and advocate of all the humanities, that great and populous city of his abode had no citizen more honored and called for, no voice more prompt and commanding. Remember that shining episode of his public life, the Sanitary Commission! Who of us, brother ministers, his survivors, can be named whose record contains a chapter like that, so replete with laborious, needful, beneficent service? Few who were not intimate with our brave brother can know what toil and cares, what runnings to and fro, what appeals to the indifferent, what wrestlings with officials, what liberal expenditure of private means that enterprise involved. And he was the soul of it all. It is not too much to say, that, although without him it would doubtless have originated, and in the hands of Olmsted and other willing and able coadjutors have done a good work, it could not without him have been the power and the success which it was. We learned from his example that the age of chivalry was not past, as Burke complained, when this new Hospitaller and Knight of St. John took the field in the cause of mercy. I visited not long since the cemetery at Arlington, where thousands upon thousands of the soldiers who fell in the war of the Rebellion are interred. As I wandered among those mostly nameless graves, I reflected that perhaps not one of that mighty host had perished without having experienced, directly or indirectly, some alleviation of his sufferings through the hand of that great charity of which our brother was the head.

And all the while, through all the years of the war, he retained his cure of All-Souls Church, preached in his pulpit, and fulfilled the duties of his pastorate.

I recall with wonder his indefatigable diligence, his

amazing activity. The steam was always up in that fierce engine that was in the body of him, of which his life was the fuel. The driving-wheel was never still. Even in his dreams, I think he must have been at work. Minister of a cultivated, intelligent, and, as one might suppose, exacting congregation, he satisfied their demands with his preaching; and yet preaching was but a small part of his activity. Often, his sermons were written at one sitting. But haste was not apparent in them. The same sermons would have cost some of us whole days in the preparation. Then, he found time for other writing in many kinds and various interests, literary and practical, spiritual and temporal, and conducted a correspondence that might have taxed the ability of a statesman. He never neglected a letter due. Indeed, writing was as natural to him as breathing. It seemed as if the pen were a part of him, a supplementary organ which Nature, foreseeing his needs, had attached to his finger-joints, and which could be sheathed or unsheathed at will. At houses where I have visited with him in his vacations, he would sit up late after the rest of us had retired, and rise before we woke, to write. It was thus that he composed his history of the Union League Club.

You will say that with all this activity, with this excessive giving out, there could be no time to take in, no time for study and reflection. As to reflection, I cannot say. Long, deep, silent, patient brooding, I suppose, was not in his nature. But this I know, he was a diligent reader. Scarcely a book of special importance in the province of history, or popular philosophy, or even fiction, was uttered by the press but he somehow found time to acquaint himself with its contents.

The one talent denied him was that of repose. He could not do nothing; he could not lie by. Of leisure he had no experience, no relish, scarcely knew what it meant. His health breaks down from overwork and he goes abroad, undertakes a grand tour for its recovery. But the tour is turned to new toil. Half the night is spent in bringing to protocol the observations and events of the day. From the railway, from the saddle, from rounds of sight-seeing, straight to the ink-stand. The written sheets are sent home, are committed to the press; and when the journey is ended, behold! it is a book. I say this not by way of commendation, but of characterization. I do not think it is the way to get the full benefit of travel. It is not even the best way to see what we "went out for to see." What we inspect only to describe on the spot we do not see to much advantage: the impression escapes with the report. To see well, one must have no ulterior end, must be passive, must let one's self be acted upon by the thing seen, —must be one's self (so to speak) the Object, and the thing seen the Subject.

But such passivity was not in Bellows's make: he must see with the will, if at all. He could not be intellectually passive and active at the same time, except occasionally in the sense in which

> "The passive master lent his hand
> To the vast soul that o'er him planned."

Occasionally. Here, I come to speak of a master-trait of our friend, a ground principle in his mental constitution, not to mention which would be a grave omission. I am at a loss by what term to express it. If I cared to be pedantic, I would say, in the Greek sense of the word, *dæmonic.* I will call it, in plain speech, an extraordinary capacity of pure inspiration. No one has really heard Bellows, no one really knew him, who has not heard him at his best on the platform. He was not always at his best, though never prosy. But when he was! We talk of extempore speech. In my experience there are two kinds : one that is good, but is not really extempore ; and one that *is* extempore, and is not good. And there is another which is miraculous, — incomparably better than anything the speaker could have possibly compassed by careful preparation or conscious effort.

"Take no care how or what ye shall speak, for it shall be given you in that same hour what ye shall speak." One must be an exceptional nature for whom this shall be a safe rule. For ordinary mortals it is a very unsafe one. I have known but two preachers in whose case it was approved ; but two who could be effectively beside themselves, who could trust their good genius to bear them better and higher than their own wit ; but two whose wings were divinely assured to them. One of these was the late Father Taylor, and the other was our Brother Bellows. With other men, their best things come to them by lonely musing ; his, in the torrent and storm of public speech. It was wondrous to listen to him in those exalted moments when fully possessed by his Dæmon, —

"Filled with fury, rapt, inspired."

You could not report those flashes with anything like a reproduction or justification of their effect, any more than you could write the aurora or stereotype the lightning. It was not so much the words themselves which he uttered as the spirit which gleamed in them and through them that thrilled you.

Of the moral qualities of this hero of our homage I need not descant to you. It might be safely assumed, did we not otherwise know it from personal acquaintance with the man and his record, that such power as he exercised and the influence that went forth of him must have had their source in great virtues. But it needs no assumption. All who knew him can testify of a moral courage which quailed at nothing, which braved all risks and defied all consequences ; a generosity which took no counsel of selfish prudence, and exceeded, as other, richer men would have reckoned, his pecuniary ability ; a tender sympathy with distress, which affliction never appealed to in vain ; a loyalty which made his friendship a prize ; a kindliness of nature which made sunshine where he came.

Such was our brother in his life and work. We do not claim for him the vision of the seer; we do not claim for him the penetration of the great original thinker, nor the erudition of the deep-read scholar, nor even the insight of the emancipated critic. What we do claim for him is a transcendent power of beneficent action. He has left no written word which, like that of Channing, has secured for itself a wide acceptance and a long future ; none which will worthily represent him to posterity. But the spirit in which he wrought, is it not immortal ? His work, shall it not survive in its fruits ? The lesson of his life, shall it not abide with us, though his place in our ranks can know him no more ? Will that place ever be filled again by one so brave and strong ? The best that can be said of any man may surely be said of him, — that he was one of those " who passing through the valley of Baca make it a well." It is good to celebrate such. It is better, so far as our meaner gifts and feebler will may suffice, to follow them.

RALPH WALDO EMERSON.

And now, Mr. President and Friends, I crave your indulgence for one more word, — a brief word *in memoriam* of another preacher of our communion, more recently deceased ; once for a few years a preacher in the technical, ecclesiastical sense, occupying a pulpit in this city as his father had done before him; always a preacher in the higher, universal sense. — a prophet, — the greatest, I think, this country or this age has known. Your thought will doubtless have anticipated me, when I name the name of Emerson.

Prevented by accident from assisting at his interment and offering my tribute with others at his bier, I desire in this presence to acknowledge the debt we owe him as promoter of the cause to which this association is vowed, — the cause of spiritual emancipation.

An emancipator he was by the positive, affirmative method, so much rarer and more effective than the negative, aggressive one adopted by most reformers. In the words of Dr. Holmes: "Here was an iconoclast without a hammer, who took down our idols from their pedestals so tenderly that it seemed like an act of worship."

Let me say, then, that Emerson, in my judgment, stands at the head of American literature in two of its most important functions: as philosophical essayist, and as lyric poet.

As philosophical essayist he is marked by absolute sincerity, independent judgment, and the freshness of original thought. His aim is not to set forth in conventional phrase the prevailing sentiment of his time, not to voice the accepted doctrine of "good society," but to face the primary fact, and to state in terms of his own what "the brooding soul" has revealed to him of the aspects and meaning of life. An original observer of Nature's plan and of human ongoings, he does not strain or strive to see and understand; he does not worry to detect the truth of things, but trustingly accepts what comes to the open sense and the waiting mind. "Stand aside and let God think" — his own memorable saying — expresses the mental process by which he gained his insight and reached his conclusions.

It was not love of singularity, as hostile critics alleged, but plain sincerity, that made his views and his writing so unconventional, and that here and there shocked propriety with some startling contradiction. It might be his misfortune, but it was not his fault, that he could not see things as others saw them. He must state them as he saw them himself. And the different view took on, as nearest his meaning, the unwonted phrase.

No writer among us has incurred more ridicule and encountered more abuse than this, our joy and our pride, in his earlier utterances. "What will this babbler say?" His speech was characterized as "the most amazing nonsense," as the raving of one who could "not put two ideas together," as sheer "blasphemy," by the Areopagites of the day, the self-constituted guardians of right thinking and good taste. The angry invectives launched against him by his censors might grieve one who prized as dearly as another the good-will of his kind; but they could not turn him from his orbit, nor baffle his serene self-possession, nor extort one syllable of wrath in reply. "Has Nature covenanted with me that I should never appear to disadvantage, never make a ridiculous figure?" "I see not any road of perfect peace which a man can travel but to take counsel of his own bosom." With such sentiments as these he steeled himself against the shafts of his adversaries, and steered "right onward."

And now, what a change! Who names him but to praise? He has created his own public. He has formed, as Wordsworth did, the taste by which he is enjoyed. Did he write: "Greatness, once and forever, has done with opinion"? He has conquered opinion. So truly he prophesied: "Let a man plant himself indomitably on his own instincts and there abide, and the huge world will come round to him."

Two streams of tendency appear in his Essays. As a philosopher he is both Platonist and Stoic: a Platonist in his contemplation of nature; a Stoic in his practical view of life. Locke still held sway when he began his career. The "Essay on the Understanding" was the text-book of philosophy in his academic years; but the whole being of the youth inclined in the opposite direction, and though not directly and at first hand conversant with the new German philosophy, he welcomed the first breathings of its spirit, which saluted him through Coleridge, and he found the fundamental principles of "transcendentalism" in his own mind. And, on the other hand, in relation to the conduct of life, as the "Meditations" of Antoninus were the favorite study of his youth, so he echoes and reproduces that imperial strain in his ethic. What more Antoninian than this: "To find the journey's end in every step of the road, to live the greatest number of good hours, is wisdom. . . . Let us be poised and wise and our own to-day. I settle myself ever firmer in the creed that we should not postpone and refer and wish, but do broad justice where we are."

A Stoic he is in the emphasis with which he affirms Right to be the absolute good, — right for its own sake, not for any foreign benefit. "There is no tax on the good of virtue, for that is the incoming of God himself, or absolute existence without any comparative." "In a virtuous action I properly *am*."

And what a triumphant optimism in his view of human nature! "Nothing shall warp me from the belief that every man is a lover of truth. There is no pure lie, no pure malignity in Nature. The entertainment of the proposition of depravity is the last profligacy and profanation.

Could it be received into the common belief, suicide would unpeople the planet."

No writer is so quotable. Scarcely a page, especially of the earlier essays, but supplies some terse and pregnant saying, worthy to be inscribed in a golden treasury of portable wisdom. And this is the signal merit of his philosophy; it gives us results instead of processes, sharp statements of weighty truths instead of long disquisitions. One pungent saying, one compact axiom that proves *itself*, is better than pages of laborious demonstration. Demonstrations we forget, but wise and witty sayings we remember; they score themselves in the brain. Force of statement, the surprise of fitness, the hitting of the nail on the head, is of Emerson's writing the distinguishing trait. No moral teacher has been so instructive to his generation.

I place Emerson at the head of the lyric poets of America. In this judgment I anticipate wide dissent; but the dissent, I think, will be less when I explain the sense in which the affirmation is intended. I do not mean that Mr. Emerson excels his competitors in poetic art. On the contrary, the want of art in his poetry may once for all be conceded. The verses often halt, the conclusion sometimes flags, and metrical propriety is recklessly violated. But the defect is closely connected with the characteristic merit of the poet, and springs from the same root, — his utter spontaneity. And this spontaneity is perhaps but a mode of that sincerity which I have noted in his prose. More than those of any of his contemporaries, his poems for the most part are inspirations. They are not made, but given; they come of themselves. They are not meditated, but burst from the soul with an irrepressible necessity of utterance, — sometimes with a rush which defies the shaping intellect.

The inspiration is not always continuous or equal

throughout; often the beginning of the poem is better than what follows. It seems as if it were not the man himself that speaks, but a power behind, — call it Dæmon or Muse. Where the Muse flags it is her fault, not his; he is not going to help her out with wilful elaboration or émendation. There is no trace, as in most poetry, of joiner-work, and no mark of the file.

Wholly unique, and transcending all contemporary verse in grandeur of style, is the piece entitled "The Problem." When first it appeared in the *Dial*, forty years ago, come July, I said: "There has been nothing done in English rhyme like this since Milton." All between it and Milton seemed tame in comparison. Some of its verses have been found worthy of a place in Westminster Abbey, the spirit of whose architecture and that of kindred temples they so fitly express.

What was said of Emerson's prose is equally true of his poetry; it is eminently quotable. More than those of any other poet of our time his lines establish themselves in the memory.

His life is a measure of the liberty wherewith he has made us free. If forty years ago one had ventured to commend him to this Association, he would have pronounced his own doom of ecclesiastical ostracism. Forty years ago he was a heretic, a blasphemer, a pest and peril to Church and State. To-day he is acknowledged a prophet, and those who reviled him are ready to garnish his sepulchre. Thus he verified his own words: "Patience and patience and patience, and we shall win at last."

As a preacher born and nurtured in our communion, he belongs to us; and I have to say of him that, as a preacher, he was one of the few in all the ages who in the realm of spirit have spoken with authority, — authority in the high sense in which the supreme Teacher from whom our Christendom dates was said to speak "as one having authority, and not as the scribes." There is an authority to which the many bow, — the authority of place, of office, the authority of tradition, of the letter, the authority of the past. His is the authority of an original, independent witness. "I am an inquirer with no past behind me." He brought a fresh eye to the contemplation of those things which most men see only through the eyes and report of others, — a vision unforestalled by precedent, unbiassed by tradition, uncontrolled by the will, unbribed by interest or passion. Such vision was possible to him through that unconditional surrender to the Spirit expressed in his saying, "Stand aside, and let God think."

To see thus was his rare privilege, to say what he saw his high calling and prophet mission. He would say only what he saw, only what he found the warrant for in his own vision and experience. Absolute sincerity in seeing and saying, — this is testimony which we must perforce respect. This is authority. He, too, could say with Jesus : "Therefore came I into the world, that I should bear witness of the truth."

The sect of Friends have a phrase, — "to live near the truth." Such living is more common with people of low estate unknown to fame than it is with men of public note. Of all distinguished men I have known, Emerson was the one who lived nearest the truth. He was truth's next neighbor, and there was nothing between. In my life-long converse with him, I could detect nothing between him and the truth, — not only no hypocrisy or pretence, but no wilfulness, no vanity, no art to win applause, no ambition even —

"That last infirmity of noble minds."

He was not covetous of speech. He had no hankering

for the ears of men. He did not go about seeking opportunities of speech, as some who are reckoned philosophers use. If he could hold his peace, he chose it rather. To be, not seem, was his intent.

When his house was burned, friends who had long waited a fit opportunity, under pretext of rebuilding it, sent him a large donation of money. In his letter of acknowledgment he wrote: "The salvages are greater than the damage." As I have looked upon him in these last years, when his power of communication was impaired by a troublesome aphasia, and have seen in his face the old serenity, the old dignity, and more than the old sweetness, it has seemed to me that the salvage was greater than the loss. A loss which he felt most keenly, but bore how patiently!

To be, not seem, is the lesson of his life. So living, he has lived down censure, has lived down ridicule, has lived down slander, oppugnance of the worthy and the unworthy, and is now accepted by us all as our best preacher of true manliness, of patience, of sincerity, of faith, of moral freedom and independence, of "whatsoever things are true, whatsoever things are honest, whatsoever things are just, whatsoever things are pure, lovely, and of good report."

> "He spoke, and words more soft than rain
> Brought the age of gold again.
> His action won such reverence sweet
> As hid all measure of the feat."

INDEX OF PERSONS.

HEBREW MEN AND TIMES

FROM THE

Patriarchs to the Messiah.

By JOSEPH HENRY ALLEN,

LECTURER ON ECCLESIASTICAL HISTORY IN HARVARD UNIVERSITY

New Edition, with an Introduction on the results of recent Old Testament criticism. Chronological Outline and Index. 16mo. Price, $1.50.

TOPICS. 1. The Patriarchs; 2. Moses; 3 The Judges; 4. David; 5. Solomon; 6. The Kings; 7. The Law; 8. The Prophets; 9. The Captivity; 10. The Maccabees; 11. The Alexandrians; 12. The Messiah.

Extract from the Preface· "... There seemed room and need of a clear, brief sketch, or outline; one that should spare the details and give the results of scholarship; that should trace the historical sequences and connections, without being tangled in questions of mere erudition, or literary discussions, or theological polemics; that should preserve the honest independence of scholarly thought, along with the temper of Christian faith; that should not lose from sight the broad perspective of secular history, while it should recognize at each step the hand of 'Providence as manifest in Israel.' Such a want as this the present volume aims to meet."

Rev. O. B. Frothingham in the Christian Examiner.

" We shall be satisfied to have excited interest enough in the theme to induce readers to take up Mr. Allen's admirable book and trace through all the richness and variety of his detail the eventful history of this Hebrew thought. His pages, with which we have no fault to find save the very uncommon fault of being too crowded and too few, will throw light on many things which must be utterly dark now to the unlearned mind; they will also revive the declining respect for a venerable people, and for a faith to which we owe much more than some of us suspect. For, however untrammelled Mr. Allen's criticism may be, his thought is always serious and reverential. And the reader of his pages, while confessing that their author has cleared away many obstructions in the way of history, will confess also that he has only made freer the access to the halls of faith. There is no light or loose or unbecoming sentence in the volume. There is no insincere paragraph. There is no heedless line. And this perhaps is one of the greatest charms of the book; for it is rare indeed that both intellect and heart are satisfied with the same letters."

Sold everywhere by all booksellers. Mailed, post-paid, by the publishers

ROBERTS BROTHERS, BOSTON.

CHRISTIAN HISTORY
IN ITS THREE GREAT PERIODS.

By JOSEPH HENRY ALLEN,
LATE LECTURER ON ECCLESIASTICAL HISTORY IN HARVARD UNIVERSITY.

First Period. "EARLY CHRISTIANITY." — TOPICS: 1. The Messiah and the Christ; 2. Saint Paul; 3. Christian Thought of the Second Century; 4. The Mind of Paganism; 5. The Arian Controversy; 6. Saint Augustine; 7. Leo the Great; 8. Monasticism as a Moral Force; 9. Christianity in the East; 10. Conversion of the Barbarians; 11. The Holy Roman Empire; 12. The Christian Schools.

Second Period. "THE MIDDLE AGE." — TOPICS: 1. The Ecclesiastical System; 2. Feudal Society; 3. The Work of Hildebrand; 4. The Crusades; 5. Chivalry; 6. The Religious Orders; 7. Heretics; 8. Scholastic Theology; 9. Religious Art; 10. Dante; 11. The Pagan Revival.

Third Period. "MODERN PHASES." — TOPICS: 1. The Protestant Reformation; 2. The Catholic Reaction; 3. Calvinism; 4. The Puritan Commonwealth; 5. Port Royal; 6. Passage from Dogma to Philosophy; 7. English Rationalism; 8. Infidelity in France; 9. The German Critics; 10. Speculative Theology; 11. The Reign of Law.

Each volume contains a Chronological Outline of its Period, with a full Table of Contents and Index, and may be ordered separately.

Volume I. ("Early Christianity") is, with a few additions, — the most important being a descriptive List of Authorities, — the same that was published in 1880, under the title, "Fragments of Christian History."

3 volumes. 16mo. Cloth. Price, $1.25 per volume.

Mr. Allen's writings, "Christian History in its Three Great Periods," 3 vols., $3.75; "Hebrew Men and Times from the Patriarchs to the Messiah," $1.50; "Our Liberal Movement in Theology chiefly as shown in Recollections of the History of Unitarianism in New England," $1.25, may be had, the five volumes, for $5.50.

Sold by all booksellers. Mailed, post-paid, on receipt of advertised price, by the publishers, ROBERTS BROTHERS, *Boston.*

Outline of Christian History.

A. D. 50-1880.

By JOSEPH HENRY ALLEN,

Author of "Hebrew Men and Times," "Christian History in its Three Great Periods," "Our Liberal Movement in Theology," etc.

16mo, Cloth.   Price, 75 Cents.

This "Outline" is designed by Mr. Allen, primarily, as a manual for class instruction. It is printed in different sizes of type, and the twelve chapters are to be studied as so many lessons, using only the portions in the larger type, — in which the general scheme or course of events are clearly stated, — after which particular periods may be studied in more detail. It is a very valuable epitome, not a history, and will be found a useful guide to more extended study of Christian history. The topics selected as lessons are the Messianic Period, the Martyr Age, Age of Controversies and Creeds, the Church and Barbarians, the Church and Feudalism, Dawn of the Modern Era, the Reformations, Wars of Religion, the English Puritans, Modern Christianity, the Nineteenth Century, and an Index of Topics and Names. — *Journal of Education.*

The little work, as its title indicates, is designed as a manual for class instruction on the origin, growth, and principles of Christianity from its foundation to the present time. It consists of twelve chapters, and each chapter is devoted to one particular epoch of Christian history. It is one of the most carefully and skilfully compiled volumes of religious history we have yet seen, and will be found invaluable to students, old as well as young. — *Saturday Evening Gazette.*

It would seem impossible to cover such a space with so limited a manual, but it is happily and ably accomplished by Mr. Allen. His three or four historical compendiums of ecclesiastical events are well known. The present handbook forms an admirable text-book for a class of young people in ecclesiastical history, and will afford to any reader a good idea of the progress of the Christian Church, with its most noted names and denominational families, during the whole period from the first century down to our days. There seems to be a marked fairness in the condensed sketches of men of different sects and their special religious movements. It is certainly a useful little manual. — *Zion's Herald.*

Sold by all Booksellers.   Mailed, post-paid, on receipt of the price, by the Publishers,

ROBERTS BROTHERS, Boston.

POSITIVE RELIGION.

ESSAYS, FRAGMENTS, AND HINTS.

By JOSEPH HENRY ALLEN,

Author of "Christian History in its Three Great Periods,"
"Hebrew Men and Times," etc.

16MO. CLOTH. PRICE, $1.25.

Among the subjects treated may be noted the following, viz.:
"How Religions Grow," "A Religion of Trust," "The World-Religions," "The Death of Jesus," "The Question of a Future Life,"
"The Bright Side," "Religion and Modern Life," etc.

The subjects are discussed, as one will indeed plainly see, by a learned Christian scholar, and from that height in life's experience which one reaches at three score and ten years. They treat of the growth of religion; of religion as an experience; of the terms "Agnostic" and "God"; of the mystery of pain, of immortality and kindred topics. The author is among the best known of the older Unitarians, and the breadth of his views, together with his modesty of statement and ripeness of judgment, give the book a charm not too common in religious works. The literary style is also pleasing. — *Advertiser.*

This little volume of 260 pages contains much that is fresh and interesting and some things which are true only from a Unitarian standpoint. It is always delightful to read an author who knows what he is writing about, and can present his thoughts in a clear and forcible manner. His intention is to exhibit religion not so much "as a thing of opinion, of emotion, or of ceremony, as an element in men's own experience, or a force, mighty and even passionate, in the world's affairs." Such an endeavor is highly laudable, and the work has been well done. — *Christian Mirror.*

A collection of a acute, reverent, and suggestive talks on some of the great themes of religion. Many Christians will dissent from his free handling of certain traditional views, dogmas of Christianity, but they will be at once with him in his love of goodness and truth, and in his contention that religion finds its complete fruition in the lives rather than the speculative opinions of men. — *N. Y. Tribune.*

Mr. Allen strikes straight out from the shoulder, with energy that shows his natural force not only unabated, but increased with added years. "At Sixty: A New Year Letter" is sweet and mellow with the sunshine of the years that bring the philosophic mind. But we are doing what we said that we must not, and must make an arbitrary end. Yet not without a word of admiration for the splendid force and beauty of many passages. These are the product of no artifice, but are uniformly an expression of that humanity which is the writer's constant end and inspiration. In proportion as this finds free and full expression, the style assumes a warmth and color that not only give an intellectual pleasure, but make the heart leap up with sympathetic courage and resolve. — *J. W. C.*

Sold everywhere.

ROBERTS BROTHERS, Publishers.

FREDERIC HENRY HEDGE'S WRITINGS.

REASON IN RELIGION.

INTRODUCTORY. — Being and Seeing, "Natural and Spiritual."
BOOK FIRST. — Religion within the Bounds of Theism.
BOOK SECOND. — Rational Christianity.

Fourth edition. 16mo. Cloth. Price $1.50.

THE PRIMEVAL WORLD OF HEBREW TRADITION.

I. The World a Divine Creation; II. Man the Image of God; III. Man in Paradise; IV. The Brute Creation; V. Paradise Lost; VI. Cain, or Property and Strife as Agents in Civilization; VII. Nine Hundred and Sixty-Nine Years; VIII. The Failure of Primeval Society; IX. The Deluge; X. Jehovah and Abraham; XII. The Heritage of the Inner Life.

Second edition. 16mo. Cloth. Price $1.50.

WAYS OF THE SPIRIT, AND OTHER ESSAYS.

I. The Way of History; II. The Way of Religion; III. The Way of Historic Christianity; IV. The Way of Historic Atonement; V. The Natural History of Theism; VI. Critique of Proofs of the Being of God; VII. On the Origin of Things; VIII. The God of Religion, or the Human God; IX. Dualism and Optimism; X. Pantheism; XI. The Two Religions; XII. The Mythical Element of the New Testament; XIII. Incarnation and Transubstantiation; XIV. The Human Soul.

Second edition. 16mo. Cloth. Price $1.50.

ROBERTS BROTHERS, PUBLISHERS,

BOSTON.